Sew Quick
Sew Cute

Fiona Goble

First published in the UK in 2014 by

Ivy Press
210 High Street
Lewes
East Sussex BN7 2NS
United Kingdom
www.ivypress.co.uk

British Library Cataloguing-in-Publication Data
A catalogue record for this book is available from the British Library

ISBN: 978-1-78240-088-2

This book was conceived, designed and produced by
Ivy Press
Creative Director Peter Bridgewater
Publisher Susan Kelly
Commissioning Editor Sophie Collins
Editorial Director Tom Kitch
Art Director James Lawrence
Design JC Lanaway
Photographer Neal Grundy
Illustrator Cathy Brear
Models Arthur Anderson, Grace Anderson, Hannah Coulson,
Ava James, Edd Lawrence, Koren Livesey, Elodie Moore, Lola Moore,
Emily Owen, Sophia Retief and Amy Sewell

Printed in China

Colour origination by Ivy Press Reprographics

10 9 8 7 6 5 4 3 2 1

Contents

Introduction 4

Kit out your sewing basket 4

Materialworld 5

All clued up 6

Projects

Tomato pincushion 8

Apple bag 12

Stash box 17

Valentine envelope 21

Tablet case 24

Phone cosy 29

Floor cushion 32

Doll-face pillows 38

Sensory play mat 45

Toy boat 50

Antarctic play set 55

Skinny-eared rabbit 60

Fabric garland 64

Christmas stockings 68

Tree star 73

Advent calendar 76

Monster draught buster 80

Bandana bib 85

Take-away cup cosy 88

Bird coasters 92

Table runner 96

Apron 100

Sarong 106

Felt sandals 111

Baby shoes 114

Lavender underwear sachet 118

Wrap skirt 122

Pompom-trimmed baby jacket 128

Strapped sundress 134

Pyjama bottoms 138

Index 143

Acknowledgements 144

Introduction

This book was written with the busy sewer in mind. The techniques are straightforward, with detailed step-by-step sequences so you can learn as you go or easily skip over anything you know already. Some projects will take no more than a couple of hours, and nothing takes longer than a weekend.

Kit out your sewing basket

Before you get going on your first project, you will need to make sure you have got everything you need. You will almost certainly have some of these items already, but there might be a few that you will need to buy.

Buying a sewing machine

If you are buying a new sewing machine, I recommend that you get a mid-priced one if you are planning to do quite a bit of sewing. It will almost certainly last longer, run more smoothly and be less noisy than a budget model.

Sewing machine A simple machine that does straight stitch and zigzag stitch is all you'll need.

Sewing machine needles Most of the projects in this book require a standard needle for sewing medium-weight fabrics. Change your needle frequently.

Dressmaking scissors For cutting fabric only.

Small scissors For trimming threads, cutting out very small fabric pieces, etc.

Ordinary scissors For cutting out paper templates.

Hand sewing needles For some projects, you will also need an embroidery needle.

Dressmaking pins For some projects, you may also need quilter's pins.

Stitch ripper and tweezers

Tape measure

Safety pins

Iron and ironing board

Water-soluble pen and quilter's pencil

Material world

There are several different types of fabric and other haberdashery items that are used in the projects. The main ones are listed below.

Cotton Most of the cotton fabrics in this book are medium-weight woven cottons, suitable for dressmaking and patchwork. Quilting fabrics are a great choice because they are available in small amounts and come in a huge variety of patterns. Remember to wash your fabric before use if it has not been pre-shrunk.

Polyester fleece The fleece fabric is usually mid-weight and is very soft and a bit stretchy. Because it is textured, it does not slip around too much and is easy to sew, even for beginners. You do not need to wash fleece before sewing as it does not shrink.

Felt Felt is a firm, non-woven fabric that is easy to sew and doesn't fray. If possible, try to buy felt that contains a percentage of wool, as it is much nicer than the 100% acrylic versions and only costs a little bit more.

Fusible bonding web Fusible bonding web is a thin web of glue, with paper on one side. It can be used to create fabric appliqués or to bond different pieces of fabric together.

You will also need

Elastic, ribbons, cord, braid and buttons for some of the projects featured in this book.

Polyester toy filling Polyester toy filling is a collection of fluffy white fibres used for stuffing toys and other handmade items. Make sure that the one you buy conforms to relevant safety standards.

Polyester wadding Polyester wadding is a bit like a sheet of polyester toy filling and is mainly used as a lightweight interlining for quilts and other padded handmade items. It is sewn in between the front and backing fabrics.

Cotton wadding Cotton wadding is used to interline fabrics to give them a bit more substance and weight. It is denser and flatter than polyester wadding.

Iron-on interfacing This is available in different weights or thicknesses. It is ironed onto the reverse of your fabric to make it stiffer and more substantial.

Threads All-purpose polyester threads are ideal for the projects in this book and come in a great range of colours. Choose a good quality thread as cheap ones tend to snap and tangle.

Tacky glue This is a special kind of PVA glue that is slightly thicker and easier to work with than standard PVA.

All clued up

There are a few basic techniques you will need to know to make sure your projects come together easily and look professional.

Preparing your templates Many of the projects will require you to use the templates provided. While it's possible to copy them by hand, it's more accurate to use a photocopier or a computer with a scanner.

To use a photocopier, simply set the copier to enlarge by the percentage listed and take a copy. If the template will be too large for the paper you are using, you will need to copy different areas and then stick the pieces together using tape. You may wish to add marks to the pattern that you can use to align the individual pieces of paper with each other.

If you are using a scanner and a computer, resize the scan to the size indicated on the pattern using your graphics editing software and then print out the scan. If the enlarged pattern is too big for your printer's paper, depending on your software and printer, you may have the option for 'tiling', in which case the template will be printed on multiple sheets that can be pieced together and secured with tape. If tiling isn't an option, you may need to divide the template into smaller sections manually, print them out onto individual sheets and then piece them together and secure them with tape.

Using fusible bonding web to create an appliqué shape Fusible bonding web is a thin web of glue on a paper backing. To use it to create an appliqué, first trace or draw your shape onto the paper side of the bonding web, using an ordinary pencil. Cut the shape out roughly then iron the bonding web glue-side down onto the reverse of your appliqué fabric. Cut the shape out and carefully peel off the backing paper. Position the appliqué on your item and iron in place before sewing.

Using fusible bonding web to line or layer fabrics You can also use bonding web to stick backing fabric to a main piece of fabric. To do this, simply iron the relevant sized piece of bonding web to the reverse of one piece of fabric. Then peel off the backing paper and iron the fabric bonding web-side down on to the reverse of your second piece of fabric.

Cutting on the bias If you look closely at a woven fabric such as woven cotton, you will see lines of thread running across and up and down the fabric. This is called the 'grain' of the fabric. Cutting on the bias means cutting across the grain, at an angle of 45 degrees. So to cut a piece on the bias, you will need to lay the template diagonally on your fabric. Pieces cut on the bias will have more flow and stretch than pieces cut in the usual way.

Cutting on the bias

Clipping curves

Topstitch

Clipping curves When you sew a curved seam on a woven fabric, you may need to make small cuts into the seam allowance so that the seam on your finished item lies flat. Use small scissors and be very careful that you do not cut into your seam.

Clipping corners When you sew a seam round a corner, it's a good idea to clip off the tip of the corner on the seam allowance. This reduces the bulk of the seam and helps make the corner look pointy. Be careful that you don't cut too near the seam.

Securing your stitches When you are machine stitching, work a few stitches backwards and forwards to secure your thread at the beginning and end of your seams. When you are hand stitching, tie a knot in your thread and work two or three stitches, one over the other, when starting your work. Work a few stitches, one over the other, to secure your thread once you have finished.

Topstitch Topstitch is simply a line of normal machine stitching that runs parallel to an edge or a seam. It helps give items a professional finish and often also helps to hold the item in shape.

Running stitch This is the simplest stitch of all and involves taking your needle in and out of your work at regular intervals. You may need to practise to make sure your stitches and the gaps between them are nice and regular.

Tacking Tacking (sometimes called 'basting') is a temporary stitch used to keep your fabric in place while you work your permanent stitching. Tacking stitches are really just big running stitches. It doesn't matter what they look like, so long as they do the job, because you will remove them once your project is complete.

Slipstitch Slipstitch is used to sew up the gaps that have been used for turning and stuffing. Fold the raw edges of the gap to the inside, in line with the seam. Run your needle about 3 mm (⅛ in.) inside the fold on one side then straight across to the inside of the fold of the other side. Repeat, working back and forth, until you come to the end of the gap.

Oversewing Oversewing is worked along the edge of a piece of fabric. You simply take your thread over the edge of the fabric then back out again about 3 mm (⅛ in.) further along.

Running stitch

Slipstitch

Oversewing

Tomato pincushion

If you're dipping your toe into the world of sewing for the first time, a pincushion is a good first project: easy *and* useful. The design is an update on a Victorian classic – in the nineteenth century, domestic accessories were often tomato-shaped, as a 'lucky' tomato on the mantelpiece of a new home was believed to bring prosperity. We've added a handful of rice in the base to give it weight and keep it upright. The pincushion is approximately 6 cm (2½ in.) high.

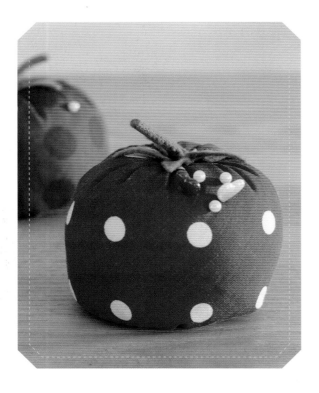

You will need

- ✂ Template on page 10
- ✂ Tracing paper and paper for template
- ✂ Pencil
- ✂ Scrap of green felt
- ✂ 12 x 24 cm (4¾ x 9½ in.) cotton fabric cut on the bias
- ✂ Green sewing thread
- ✂ Thread to match your fabric
- ✂ Handful of rice or lentils (optional)
- ✂ Handful of polyester toy filling
- ✂ Basic sewing kit (see page 4)
- ✂ Water-soluble pen

How to make the tomato pincushion

{1} Using the template below, cut out the leaf shape from green felt and cut out a 2 x 3-cm (¾ x 1⅛-in.) rectangle of felt for the stalk.

{2} Check that your main fabric has been cut on the bias (see page 6). Fold your main fabric in half widthways, right sides together. Taking a 1-cm (⅜-in.) seam allowance, machine stitch the short edges together. Press the seam open.

{3} With your machine set on the longest stitch possible, machine along one of the long edges, securing your thread at one end only and leaving a reasonably long length of thread free at the other end.

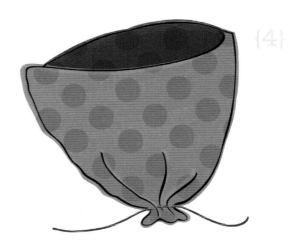

{4} Pull on the free end of thread to gather the lower edge and machine stitch through the gathers a few times to secure very firmly. Your fabric will now have formed a cup shape. Turn the piece right side out.

Template
Shown at actual size.

5 cm (2 in.)

5.2 cm (2¹⁄₁₆ in.)

{5}

{5} Place a handful of rice or lentils into the pincushion, if required, and then a handful of polyester toy filling.

{7}

Stuffing your pincushion

To keep your needles and pins in tip-top sharp condition, you may want to fill the top part of your pincushion with fine steel wool or emery sand (some people also swear by aquarium sand). A number of experienced sewers also recommend wool scraps to help the pins stay smooth.

{6}

{6} Using a doubled length of thread, work a line of hand running stitch (see page 7) around the top edge of the pincushion, 1 cm (⅜ in.) from the raw edge. Pull up tightly, tuck the raw edge in, and stitch through the gathered fabric a few times to make it really secure.

{7} Hand sew the leaf to the top of the tomato at the centre. Roll the small rectangle of felt for the stalk into a long, thin tube and oversew the edge in place (see page 7). Stitch the stalk to the centre of the leaf. If you want to, take your thread right the way through the base of your pincushion and back up again before securing. This gives your pincushion a nice squashy look and will make it feel firmer.

Apple bag

If you need a decent-sized tote bag that is strong enough to hold books, papers and everything else you need during a busy day, then this one will fit the bill. The outside pockets are deep enough to hold small items without any danger of them dropping out, too. This example is made from a soft grey wool flannel with some boldly printed quilting cotton fabric for the lining. Check that your chosen lining does not have a directional pattern, or it won't work with this design. For a more summery look, you could try a medium-weight denim instead of the flannel.

You will need

- ✂ Two 38 x 69-cm (15 x 27-in.) pieces of pale grey wool flannel fabric
- ✂ Two 38 x 71-cm (15 x 28-in.) pieces of co-ordinating printed cotton fabric for lining
- ✂ 10 x 130 cm (4 x 51 in.) pale grey wool flannel fabric for strap
- ✂ Pale grey sewing thread
- ✂ Thread to match your patterned fabric (if necessary)
- ✂ One 32-mm (1¼-in.) brown button
- ✂ Lime green sewing thread to secure the button
- ✂ Basic sewing kit (see page 4)
- ✂ Water-soluble pen

Finished size

Bag: 35 cm (14 in.) wide by
39 cm (15½ in.) tall
Strap: 114 cm (45 in.) from the top
of one side of the bag to the other

How to make the apple bag

{1} Place the two pale grey rectangles right sides together and machine stitch down the two long sides, taking a 1-cm (⅜-in.) seam allowance. Press the seams open. Repeat with the printed cotton rectangles. You will now have two tube shapes, which are open at both ends.

{2} Turn the patterned cotton tube right side out and insert it into the grey tube so that the side seams match and the raw edges along the tube openings meet at one end. Pin the tubes together around this opening, then machine stitch the pieces, taking a 1-cm. (⅜-in.) seam allowance.

{3} Turn the grey part right side out, so that you now have what looks like one long tube of fabric. Tuck the patterned fabric part of the tube into the grey part, so that the seam joining the two fabrics is on the inside of the doubled tube, 1.5 cm (⅝ in.) down from the folded edge. Machine stitch along the seam line where the two fabrics meet to secure the pieces in position. This will be the top edge of your bag.

{4} At the opposite end of the tube, fold the patterned fabric under by 1.5 cm (⅝ in.) and press. Fold the fabric under by another 1.5 cm (⅝ in.) and press again. Place the folded edge over the grey fabric so that the raw edge of the grey fabric touches the inside of the fold of the patterned fabric, and pin in place. Machine stitch along the inner folded edge of the patterned fabric in matching thread. This edge will form the top edge of the pockets on the finished bag.

{5} Pin the side seams of the two tubes together for about 20 cm (8 in.) from the pocket edge upwards (this keeps the fabric in place for the next stage). Measure 24 cm (9½ in.) up from the finished pocket edge at both sides of the tube. Using the water-soluble pen, draw a straight line across the bag between these two marks, then machine stitch across this line. Remove the pins from the side seam.

{6} Fold the pocket edge part of the bag upwards all the way around the bag, so that the line you have just sewn forms the base of the bag and the pockets begin to take shape. Press lightly and pin the pocket part to the main part of the bag at the sides. On one side of the bag, using the water-soluble pen, draw two vertical lines on the pocket part, each one 12 cm (4¾ in.) from each side seam. On the other side of the bag, draw one vertical line in the centre of the pocket piece. Pin along these lines through all four layers of fabric to keep your fabric smooth for the next stage (not into all eight layers). Then machine stitch along all the lines to form the pocket dividers.

{7} At both bag side seams, machine stitch a short line of stitching from the top edge of the pocket part to the horizontal line of stitching around the pocket edge. (This will make sure the pockets look neat and stay in position.)

{8} Fold the grey strip that will form the bag strap in half lengthways, so that the right sides are together. Machine stitch along the long raw edges, taking a 1-cm (⅜-in.) seam allowance. Turn up 1.5 cm (⅝ in.) along the two short edges and press. Turn the tube right side out through one of the short ends and press so that the seam lies on the inside, along one of the long edges.

{9} Machine stitch around all four edges of the strap, 6 mm (¼ in.) in from the outside edge.

{10} Pin the strap to the sides of the bag on the inside, so that the strap lies over the side seams and the short edge of the strap lies 7.5 cm (3 in.) down from the top edge of the bag. Box stitch the strap to the bag, working the top edge of the box over the stitching around the top edge of the bag and the lower edge over the top stitching on the strap.

{11} Using contrasting lime green thread, sew the button in place at the top of the stitching that separates the two pockets on one side of the bag.

Stash box

Any keen maker needs a stash box, or several, to keep all their essential
bits and pieces in order, be they knitting yarns, odds and ends of fabric, or crucial
ribbons and trimmings. At 20 cm (8 in.) tall, the box shown here is quite roomy
– but you can easily alter the dimensions of your pieces to create a complete stash
storage system, with a range of boxes of different sizes. The handles are optional.

You will need

- ✂ 46 cm (18 in.) cotton fabric, 114 cm (45 in.) wide, for outer part
- ✂ 46 cm (18 in.) cotton fabric, 114 cm (45 in.) wide, for lining
- ✂ 46 cm (18 in.) heavyweight iron-on interfacing, 91 cm (36 in.) wide
- ✂ One 76-cm (30-in.) square of cotton wadding for interlining
- ✂ Sewing thread to match your fabrics
- ✂ Basic sewing kit (see page 4)

How to make the stash box

{1} From your main fabric (i.e. the fabric for the outer part), cut out one 30-cm (12-in.) square for the base, four 22 x 30-cm (8¾ x 12-in.) rectangles for the sides and two 7.5 x 18-cm (3 x 7-in.) rectangles for the handles. From the lining fabric, cut out a base and four sides, matching the sizes of the main fabric. From the iron-on interfacing, cut out a base, four sides and two handle pieces, also matching the sizes of the main fabric.

{2} With right sides together and aligning the raw edges, place one of the main fabric side pieces on the base. (If your fabric has a directional pattern, like ours, make absolutely sure that you seam the *lower* edge of your side piece to the base, otherwise the pattern on your finished box will be upside down!) Machine stitch together, taking a 1-cm (⅜-in.) seam allowance and beginning and ending your seam 1 cm (⅜ in.) from the raw edges. Repeat on the opposite side. Press the seams open.

{3} Machine stitch the two other side pieces to the other sides of the base in the same way, leaving a 10-cm (4-in.) gap in the centre of one side for turning the bag right-way out after you have sewn the lining in.

{4} Bring two adjacent side pieces right sides together so that the raw edges meet. Machine stitch them together, taking a 1-cm (⅜-in.) seam allowance. Join the remaining sides in the same way.

{5} Iron the interfacing pieces to the reverse of your lining pieces. Machine stitch the lower edges of the side lining pieces to the base lining piece, as in steps 2 and 3 – but do not leave a gap in one of the seams.

{6} Lay your lining piece face up on the cotton wadding, pin in position and sew all around the lining piece very close to the edge. Trim away the excess wadding. Complete the lining piece in the same way as in step 4.

{7} Iron the interfacing pieces for the handles onto the reverse of the main fabric pieces. Fold in 1 cm (⅜ in.) along the two long sides of both handle pieces and press. Then fold the two long sides together and press. Machine stitch close to the edge along the two long edges of the handle.

{8} Pin the handles in place at the top of the right side of the box, aligning the raw edges. The edges of the handles should be 8 cm (3¼ in.) from the corner of the box. The long edge where the seam allowance has been folded in should be on the outside of the handle.

{10} Turn the box right side out through the hole in the base of the outer piece. Slipstitch the gap in the base closed (see page 7).

{9} With right sides together, matching the seams and aligning the top raw edges, place the lining in the outer box. Pin around the edges, then machine stitch around the top, taking a 1.5-cm (⅝-in.) seam allowance, stitching backwards and forwards over the handles to make sure they're securely fixed (see page 7).

{11} Press the sides and base of the box, taking particular care around the top edge so that the seam between the lining and outer fabric runs evenly along the top of the box. Topstitch around the top edge of the box, 1 cm (⅜ in.) down from the edge (see page 7).

Valentine envelope

If you want to impress on Valentine's day, the wrapping is almost as important as the present. Fabric envelopes for small gifts are a fast-growing fashion and you can buy any number of designs in the shops – but it's much nicer to make something unique to reflect the thought behind your gift. The example here is 13 cm (5 in.) square – big enough to hold all manner of treats, from sweets to jewellery, yet still small enough to look cute. The size can easily be altered, though, to suit your own Valentine's offering.

You will need

- ✂ Template on right
- ✂ Tracing paper and paper to make templates
- ✂ Pencil
- ✂ 23-cm (9-in.) square of printed cotton fabric for the outer part of the envelope
- ✂ 23-cm (9-in.) square of plain white linen fabric for the lining
- ✂ 23-cm (9-in.) square of fusible bonding web
- ✂ 7 x 10 cm (2¾ x 4 in.) bright pink felt and a matching piece of fusible bonding web
- ✂ Snap fastener, 1 cm (⅜ in.) in diameter
- ✂ White round button, 18 mm (1¹⁄₁₆ in.) in diameter
- ✂ White heart-shaped button, 18 mm (1¹⁄₁₆ in.) tall
- ✂ Thread to match your main fabric and felt
- ✂ Basic sewing kit (see page 4)
- ✂ Water-soluble pen

Template

Shown at 33% – enlarge by 300% for actual size.

position of hand

21 cm (8¼ in.)

21 cm (8¼ in.)

How to make the valentine envelope

{1}

{1} Press the square of fusible bonding web glue side down onto the reverse of your main fabric (see page 6). Peel the paper backing off the bonding web and press the main fabric down onto the reverse of your lining fabric.

{2} Prepare your envelope template following the instructions on page 6 and cut it out. Lay the template on the lining side of your stiffened fabric. Draw around it with the water-soluble pen and cut it out.

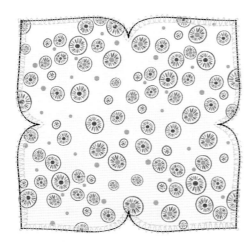

{3} Zigzag stitch around the entire shape using your sewing machine.

{4} Using the smaller piece of bonding web and the pink felt, prepare the appliqué motif (see page 6). Cut the appliqué motif out and apply it to the centre of the envelope shape. Hand sew around the edge of the hand in a small running stitch, using matching thread (see page 7).

{5} Fold the sides of the envelope into the centre and the lower edge upwards, in line with the inner corners, and press. Secure in place by working around the sides of the lower edge in a hand running stitch, along the inner edge of the zigzag stitching. Sew the top part of the snap fastener on the wrong side of the top point of the envelope, about 1 cm (⅜ in.) down from the tip of the point. Sew the base of the snap fastener on the right side of the lower part of the envelope to correspond. Sew the round button in position on the right side of the top point of the envelope, so that it corresponds with the snap fastener.

{6} Sew the heart-shaped button in position in the centre of the hand.

Tablet case

Thick and soft, felt is available at every craft shop or online supplier in a rainbow array of colours and at very reasonable prices. Choose two favourite shades to create this custom-made case to keep your precious tablet safe from accidental bangs and scrapes. Although the case has got several layers, the making method is simple and doesn't involve any fiddly turning. And once you've completed it, you can follow the same steps to create a case for your e-reader or any other slim gadget.

You will need

- ✂ 31 x 51 cm (12 x 20 in.) purple felt
- ✂ 23 x 31 cm (9 x 12 in.) grey felt
- ✂ 4 x 8-cm (1½ x 3¼-in.) scrap of pink felt
- ✂ 30 x 59 cm (12 x 23 in.) cotton fabric
- ✂ Fusible bonding web
- ✂ 30 x 59 cm (12 x 23 in.) thin (60-g/2-oz) polyester wadding
- ✂ Two white buttons, 18 mm (¾ in.) in diameter
- ✂ 60-cm (24-in.) length of olive green embroidery thread
- ✂ Thread to match the purple felt
- ✂ Cream thread
- ✂ Basic sewing kit (see page 4)
- ✂ Paper for the template
- ✂ Pencil
- ✂ Water-soluble pen

How to make the tablet case

{1} To make your templates, draw around your tablet remembering to keep your pencil vertical. Add a 1-cm (⅜-in.) seam allowance all around and ignore any rounded corners. Cut out the template. Draw around the template on a second piece of paper and cut out another rectangle. With the template facing you so that it is wider than it is tall, fold one lower corner up to the top edge, then unfold. Do the same with the other corner and unfold again. The folds on your paper should now show two triangles, one slightly larger than the other. Cut out the larger of the triangles to form the second part of your template and discard the remains of the paper. Trim the point of the triangle where the two equal sides meet to round it off.

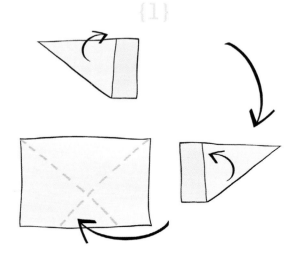

{2} Using your templates and water-soluble pen, cut out the following:
- ✂ one triangle and one house-shaped piece from the purple felt (use the triangle and rectangle combined to make the house shape) and one rectangle from the grey felt.
- ✂ two pieces of bonding web for both the house and the rectangle shape and a single piece of bonding web for the triangle shape.
- ✂ one rectangle and one house shape from wadding and from the cotton lining fabric.

{3} Trim off 6 mm (¼ in.) around the entire edge of the two pieces of wadding, so that they are exactly the same shape but are slightly smaller than the felt pieces.

{4} Iron one of the house-shaped pieces of bonding web glue side down onto the felt house shape (see page 6). Iron the other house-shaped piece of bonding web onto the house-shaped piece of lining fabric. Peel the backing paper off both pieces of bonding web. Sandwich the house-shaped wadding between the felt and lining pieces and press in place. You will need to press the piece on both the lining side and the felt side and around the edges to make sure that your 'sandwich' is secure.

{5} Repeat step 4 to make the rectangular part of your case.

{6} Apply the triangle of bonding web to the triangle of felt and press in place. Peel the backing paper off the triangle and press it onto the felt side of the rectangle. On your sewing machine, work straight stitch around the two equal sides of the triangle 5 mm (³⁄₁₆ in.) from the edge. Then zigzag stitch around these sides between the straight stitching and the raw edge of the triangle.

{7} On your sewing machine, straight stitch across the top of the rectangle, 1 cm (³⁄₈ in.) from the edge. Trim the edge so that there is 5 mm (³⁄₁₆ in.) of fabric above the stitching. Zigzag stitch along the top of the rectangle between the straight stitching and the raw edge of the rectangle.

{8} With wrong sides together and the base of the triangle at the lower edge of the house-shaped piece, place the rectangle on the house-shaped piece. Pin the pieces in place. On your machine, straight stitch around the outer edge, including the pointed part of the house-shaped piece, taking a 1-cm (⅜-in.) seam allowance. Trim the seam allowance to 5 mm (³⁄₁₆ in.). Zigzag stitch around the outer edges of the entire piece between the straight stitching and the raw edge.

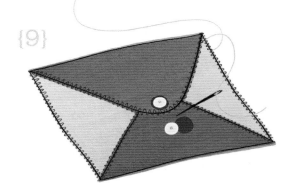

{9} Cut out two circles of pink felt, both slightly larger than your buttons (you can use a larger button as your template or any small round object of the right size). Place the felt circles under the buttons and, using cream thread, sew one button in place on the corner of the top flap and the other onto the main case, so that the felt circle comes just below the corner of the top flap when it is folded down.

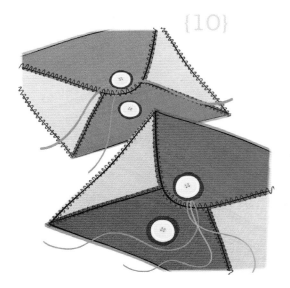

{10} Find the centre of the length of embroidery thread and tie it around the top button. Divide the thread into three groups so that there are four strands in each group. Plait the thread. When you are near the end, tie the three groups of thread together and trim the knot. Wrap the plaited cord in a figure of eight around the two buttons to secure the case.

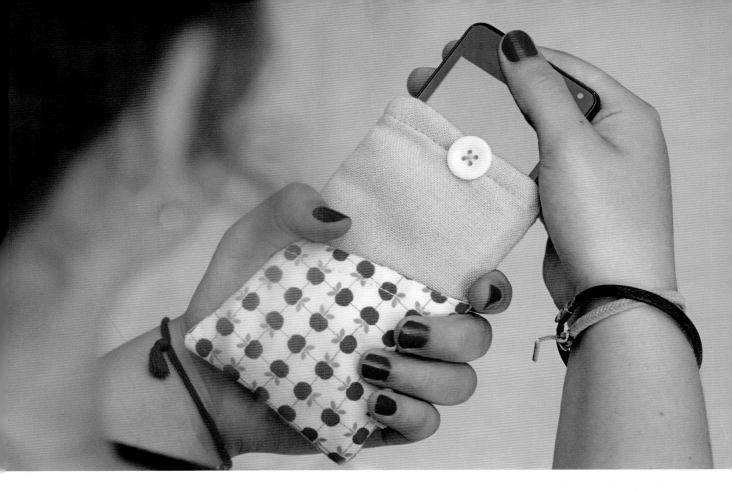

Phone cosy

5–8 hrs

There are dozens of phone cases available in everything from leather to plastic, but you can create a good-looking protective, and unique, case for your mobile, customized to your own taste, very easily. This pattern is fleece-lined to protect your phone but the outer sleeve can be made from whatever fabric you like – plain or patterned, flat or textured. Our version has a small pocket incorporated – handy for headphones or even bank or business cards – and it hooks shut with a simple button-and-elastic-loop device. The fleece lining has a slight grip effect, which means that your phone isn't likely to s ip out of its case accidentally.

You will need

- Paper for template
- Pencil
- 20-cm (8-in.) square of plain heavyweight cotton or linen fabric
- 20-cm (8-in.) square of co-ordinating fleece for the lining
- 10 x 20 cm (4 x 8 in.) printed cotton for the pocket
- 10-cm (4-in.) square of medium-weight iron-on interfacing
- Threads to match your fabrics
- Thin hair elastic to match your plain fabric (or coloured elastic cord)
- White button, 18 mm (¾ in.) in diameter
- Basic sewing kit (see page 4)
- Water-soluble pen

How to make the phone cosy

{1} To prepare your main template, trace round your phone, taking care to hold your pencil at a right angle. Add 1.5 cm (⅝ in.) all around to allow for the seam allowance and the thickness of the phone, and ignore all rounded corners. Cut out the template.

{2} To prepare the pocket template, draw around your main template, then draw a line across the template at the halfway point. On the right-hand side, measure up 2.5 cm (1 in.) from the halfway line. Join this point to the halfway point on the left to form the top edge of the pocket. Cut out the template.

{3} Using the main template, cut out two pieces from your outer fabric and two pieces from the fleece. Trim the two fleece pieces so that they are 1 cm (⅜ in.) shorter and 6 mm (¼ in.) narrower than the outer pieces. Cut out two pocket pieces from your pocket fabric, one using the template the right way up and one using it face down. Cut one pocket piece from the interfacing. Also cut out a rectangle of outer fabric measuring 4.5 x 5 cm (1¾ x 2 in.) for the tab.

{4} For the tab, fold the fabric under 6 mm (¼ in.) along both the long edges, then fold the piece in half lengthways. Machine stitch close to the folded edges and press in half widthways.

{5} Iron the interfacing onto the wrong side of one of the pocket pieces. Place the two pocket pieces right sides together and machine stitch along the sloping edge, taking a 1-cm (⅜-in.) seam allowance. Turn right side out and press carefully, so that the seam runs along the centre of the sloping edge. Topstitch 7 mm (¼ in.) down from the sloping edge (see page 7).

{6} Pin the pocket to the right side of one of the outer pieces, so that the pocket slopes upwards from left to right. Pin the tab in place on top of the pocket piece, so that the base of the tab is 3 cm (1⅛ in.) up from the lower edge. The folded edge of the tab should face inwards and the raw edges should line up with the raw edges of the main piece.

{7} Machine tack the elastic cord loop in place just either side of the centre on the right side of the second main piece (the piece without the pocket). The tacking should be 1 cm (⅜ in.) from the raw edge and the loop should be about 1.5 cm (⅝ in.) long.

{8} Pin the two outer pieces right sides together and machine stitch around the sides and base, taking a 1-cm (⅜-in.) seam allowance. Clip the corners (see page 7).

{9} Pin the two fleece pieces right sides together. Machine stitch around the sides and base, taking a 1-cm (⅜-in.) seam allowance and leaving a 4-cm (1½-in.) gap in the centre of the lower edge for turning. Trim the seam allowances and clip the corners. Turn the right way out.

{10} Place the fleece lining inside the outer part of the case (still wrong-way out), making sure the pieces are right sides together and that the side seams match. Machine stitch around the top, taking a 1-cm (⅜-in.) seam allowance, stitching backwards and then forwards again over the elastic loop to make sure that it is really secure (see page 7).

{11} Turn the case right side out through the gap in the fleece lining, making sure that the pocket is on the correct side. Press the outer part of the case carefully and then hand slipstitch the gap in the lining closed (see page 7). Push the lining down into the main case.

{12} Topstitch (see page 7) around the top of the case 6 mm (¼ in.) from the top edge. Sew the button in place, making sure it corresponds with the elastic loop.

Floor cushion

5-8 hrs

Floor cushions are a good answer to any temporary seating shortage, whether in a TV den or a teenager's bedroom. This one does double-duty as extra storage – it's cunningly stuffed with a spare duvet, which can be pulled out for an impromptu sleepover. The floor cushion needs to be made from an upholstery-weight fabric. The quantities in the materials list allow for using a directionally patterned fabric; if your choice is plain, or has a non-directional pattern, such as a polka dot, you may need slightly less.

You will need

- ✂ Templates on page 37
- ✂ Tracing paper and paper for templates
- ✂ Pencil
- ✂ 2.3 m (2½ yd) fabric 110 cm (43 in.) wide or 1.6 m (1¾ yd) fabric 150 cm (59 in.) wide
- ✂ Thread to match your fabric
- ✂ 46-cm (18-in.) closed-end general-purpose zip to match your fabric
- ✂ Single duvet for stuffing
- ✂ Basic sewing kit (see page 4)
- ✂ Water-soluble pen
- ✂ Ruler
- ✂ Stitch ripper

How to make the floor cushion

{1} Using the templates on page 37, cut out one top piece, two base pieces and five side pieces. If your fabric is directional like ours, when cutting the base pieces, remember to cut one semi-circle with the template the right way up and one semi-circle with the template face down. You must also make sure that your pattern is the right way up on the side pieces, with the base of the pattern at the broader, lower end of the shape. For the handle, cut out a rectangle measuring 8 x 23 cm (3¼ x 9 in.).

{2} Use your sewing machine to zigzag stitch around all the pieces except for the handle.

{3} Pin the five side pieces right sides together and machine stitch, taking a 1.5-cm (⅝-in.) seam allowance. Then stitch the first and fifth side pieces together, again taking a 1.5-cm (⅝-in.) seam allowance. Press all the seams open.

{1}

{3}

{4} Pin the two base pieces right sides together and measure 11 cm (4½ in.) in from each end of the straight edge. Mark these points with the water-soluble pen.

{5} Taking a 1.5-cm (⅝-in.) seam allowance and using a standard-length straight stitch, sew from one outer edge to the first marker, securing your stitching at the beginning and end by working a few stitches backwards then forwards again (see page 7). Change your machine to the longest stitch possible and sew to the second marker. Then secure your thread by working a few stitches forwards then backwards at the second marker and sew to the end using a standard-length straight stitch. Press the seam open.

{6} Lay the zip face down over the centre part of the seam (where you have sewn the large stitches) on the wrong side of your work and pin in place. Machine stitch the zip in place by working a slim rectangle all around it. You will need to move the zipper mechanism as you sew to make sure that your stitching is smooth.

{7} With the right side of your work facing, use your stitch ripper to undo the large stitches running down the centre of the zip, between the markers.

{8} Fold the handle piece in half lengthways, right sides together, and machine stitch along the long edges, taking a 1-cm (⅜-in.) seam allowance. Turn the handle right side out. Fold in 1 cm (⅜ in.) along each of the short edges and press the handle so that the long seam runs along the middle of the handle. Sew a line of stitching close to the edge around the entire handle.

{9} Pin the handle right side up in the centre of the top piece of the floor cushion. Measure up 2.5 cm (1 in.) from each end of the stitching on the short edges of the handle and, using the water-soluble pen, draw a line across the handle. Use these lines as a guide to secure the handle by machine stitching a square with a box stitch inside at each end.

{10} With right sides together, pin the sides to the base. Machine stitch, taking a 1.5-cm (⅝-in.) seam allowance.

{11} Open the zip in the base piece. With right sides together, pin the top to the sides. Machine stitch, taking a 1.5-cm (⅝-in.) seam allowance.

{12} Turn the cushion cover right side out through the open zip and press. Insert the duvet into the cover and close the zip.

Templates
Shown at 20% – enlarge by 500% for actual size.

Bottom piece

36 cm (14 in.)

67.5 cm (26¾ in.)

Top piece

place along fold of fabric

47.5 cm (18¾ in.)

23.5 cm (9⅜ in.)

Side piece

40 cm (15½ in.)

45 cm (17½ in.)

Doll-face pillows

This pair of pillows, inspired by a set of painted wooden Scandinavian dolls, is an ideal choice to liven up kids' bedrooms. The fronts are made from felt with appliquéd features and the backs are made from polyester fleece to give them a nice soft feel. Once you've made one pair, you can invent a whole range of characters – changing the hair, eyes and so on by varying the shapes and colours of the appliqués.

You will need

For each pillow

✂ Templates on pages 43–44

✂ Pencil

✂ 55 x 117 cm (21½ x 46 in.) pale pink felt

✂ 41 x 80 cm (16 x 31½ in.) light mauve polyester fleece fabric

✂ Small piece of light pink polyester fleece or felt for the cheeks

✂ Small piece of black felt for the eyes

✂ 20-cm (8-in.) square of fusible bonding web

✂ 38-cm (15-in.) circular pillow pad

✂ Dark grey embroidery thread

✂ Light pink and mauve sewing threads

✂ Pair of compasses

✂ Basic sewing kit (see page 4)

For the man pillow

✂ 20 x 41 cm (8 x 16 in.) dark brown flannel or felt

✂ Small piece of red felt for the mouth

✂ Dark brown and red sewing threads

For the woman pillow

✂ 31 x 41 cm (12 x 16 in.) grey flannel or felt

✂ Small piece of bright pink felt for the mouth

✂ Grey and bright pink sewing threads

How to make the doll-face pillows

{1} To make the templates for the pillow front and the two pieces that make up each pillow back, use the compass and pencil to draw three circles, each 38 cm (15 in.) in diameter. Cut out one whole circle for the pillow front. For the back pieces, cut the circles as shown, remembering to straighten the sides of the lower edge of the inner back piece (this will help make sure the hem on this piece is really neat).

{2} Use the front template to cut out the front of each pillow from pale pink felt. Also cut a strip of pale pink felt measuring 10 x 115 cm (4 x 45 in.) for the side strip of the pillow. Cut out the two back pieces for each pillow from the fleece fabric.

{3} Using the templates on pages 43–44, cut out the hairpieces from dark brown flannel or felt for the man's hair and grey flannel or felt for the woman's hair.

{4} Trace the templates from pages 43–44 for two sets of facial features – the eyes, nose, cheeks and mouth – and the moustache for the man onto the backing paper of the piece of fusible bonding web. Cut out the shapes on the bonding web roughly, not too close to the pencil outlines. Iron the bonding web onto the reverse side of the appropriate fabrics (check the photo on page 38–39), remembering to have your iron on a fairly low setting (see page 6).

{5} Peel the backing paper off the face appliqués and position them on the fronts of the pillows, using the photographs as a guide. Use the hairpieces to help you position the features, but do not attach them just yet. Once you are happy with their positions, iron the facial features in place, again remembering to have your iron on a fairly low setting.

{6} Work hand running stitch (see page 7) around the noses using light pink thread. For the man, work running stitch around the edge of the mouth, using red sewing thread. For the woman, oversew the mouth in place around the inner and outer circles using bright pink sewing thread (see page 7). On both pillows, machine stitch around the cheeks, just in from the edges, using zigzag stitch and light pink thread. Using two strands of dark grey embroidery thread, hand sew six straight stitches out from the centre of the eye to just over the edge – the stitches should form a star shape over the eye. For the woman, use three strands of dark grey embroidery thread to work three straight stitches above each eye for eyelashes. For the man, machine stitch around the moustache using zigzag stitch and brown sewing thread.

{7} Pin the hairpieces in position and machine stitch them in place along the inside parts only with zigzag stitch, using matching thread.

{8} Fold each side strip in half widthways. Using matching thread and taking a 1-cm (⅜-in.) seam allowance, machine stitch the two short edges together. The side strips will now be a circle. Press the seam open.

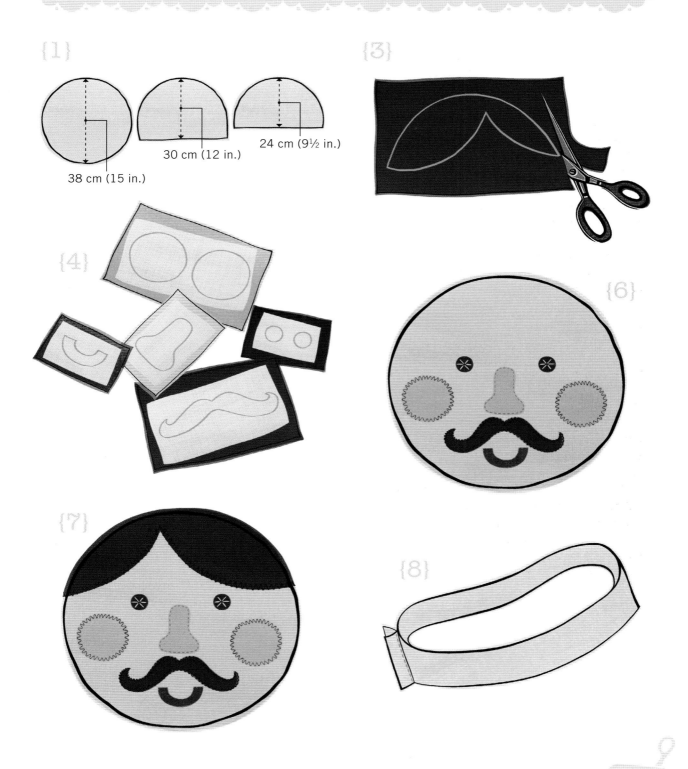

{1}

38 cm (15 in.)

30 cm (12 in.)

24 cm (9½ in.)

{3}

{4}

{6}

{7}

{8}

{9} With right sides together, pin one long edge of a side strip around the outer edge of the front of each pillow, placing the seam of the side strip at the top of the head. Using light pink thread and taking a 1-cm (⅜-in.) seam allowance, machine stitch the strips in place.

{10} Fold under 3 cm (1⅛ in.) along the straight edges of one of the back pieces. Pin in position, then work a machine zigzag stitch along the raw edge to secure the edge in place. Repeat for the other back piece.

{11} With right sides together, pin the outer back piece of each pillow (the smaller piece) to the side strip, so that the straight edge of the back piece goes across the centre of the face, from one side to the other. Now pin the inner back piece (the larger piece) right side down to the side strip, so that its straight edge overlaps the straight edge of the other outer piece. Using light pink thread and taking a 1-cm (⅜-in.) seam allowance, machine stitch the back pieces to the side piece by sewing around the entire outside edge.

{12} Turn the pillow covers right side out and insert the pillow pads.

Template

Shown at 40% – enlarge by 250% for actual size.

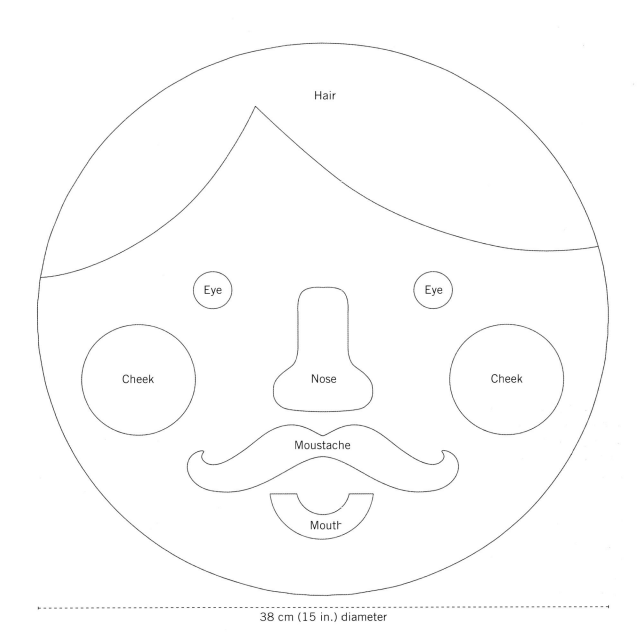

Hair

Eye   Eye

Cheek   Nose   Cheek

Moustache

Mouth

38 cm (15 in.) diameter

Template

Shown at 40% – enlarge by 250% for actual size.

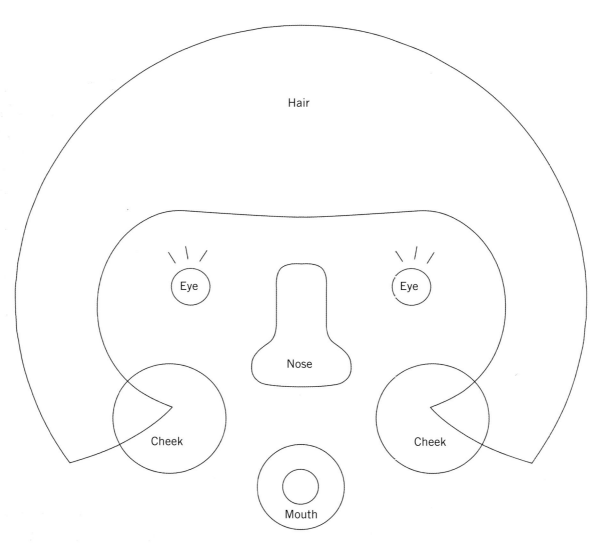

Hair

Eye

Eye

Nose

Cheek

Cheek

Mouth

38 cm (15 in.) diameter

Sensory play mat

Help the baby in your life begin to get accustomed to all the textures and sounds surrounding them with a homemade play mat that offers a range of different sensations. The petals are made from an assortment of fabrics, including towelling, velour, cotton waffle and fleece – so each petal looks or feels different. Crinkly cellophane, bells and a squeaker were sewn inside separate petals for a bit of added fun for the baby to explore. The play mat measures about 142 cm (56 in.) across. With supervision, the mat is suitable for babies from birth to around 15 months.

You will need

- ✂ Template on page 47
- ✂ Paper for template
- ✂ 110-cm (43-in.) square of fabric for the flower centre
- ✂ 110-cm (43-in.) square of fleece fabric for the backing
- ✂ 110-cm (43-in.) square of 125-g (4-oz) polyester wadding
- ✂ Eight assorted fabrics measuring approximately 41 x 61 cm (16 x 24 in.) for each of the eight petals; I used four plain-coloured textured fabrics and four co-ordinating printed cottons
- ✂ Sewing thread to match your fabrics
- ✂ 280 g (10 oz) polyester toy filling
- ✂ Squeaker, bells and crinkly cellophane to put inside some of the petals
- ✂ 76-cm (30-in.) length of string
- ✂ Water-soluble pen and quilter's pencil
- ✂ Ruler
- ✂ Long quilter's safety pins
- ✂ Basic sewing kit (see page 4)

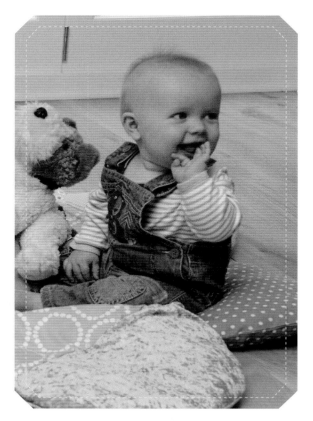

How to make the play mat

{1}

{1} To draw the large octagon for the main part of the play mat, tie one end of your string around the water-soluble pen and the other around the quilter's pencil. The length of string between the pencil and pen should be approx. 51 cm (20 in.). Lay your flower centre fabric out on a large surface or the floor. Holding the quilter's pencil at the centre of your fabric and keeping the string taut, move the water-soluble pen right around the pencil to draw a large circle. Cut out the circle.

{2} Fold the flower centre piece of fabric in quarters and mark each quarter at the edge. Fold each quarter in half and mark the centre points. You should now have eight marks around the edge of your fabric.

{3} Draw a straight line from one mark to the next all around the fabric edge and cut along these lines to make an octagon. Lay the flower centre on top of your backing fabric and use it as a template to cut out another octagon. Cut an octagon of wadding out in the same way.

{4} Use the template, see right, to make the petals. If you want to make sure the size at the bottom edge of the petal matches the section of the octagonal flower center it will be attached to, measure across the octagonal section, 1 cm (⅜ in.) from the outer edge, then add 2 cm (¾ in.) to this measurement. This will give you the correct measurement for the bottom edge of the petal for that particular section.

Template

Shown at 20% – enlarge by 500% for actual size. To make sure the curves are even, fold the paper in half first along the centre vertical line.

29 cm (11½ in)

40 cm (15½ in.)

{5} For each of the eight petals, fold each piece of fabric in half, pin the template on top and cut out two petal pieces in the same fabric. Place the two pieces right sides together and machine stitch around the curved edge, taking a 1-cm (⅜-in.) seam allowance.

{7} Stuff all the petals lightly and evenly with polyester toy filling; each petal should be about 12.5–4 cm (1–1½ in.) thick. Insert the squeaker, bells and crinkly cellophane into the chosen petals; I put them into the petals made from printed cottons rather than the ones made from textured fabric. If necessary, wrap the squeaker and bells in scraps of wadding before you put them into the petals, to help them stay in place.

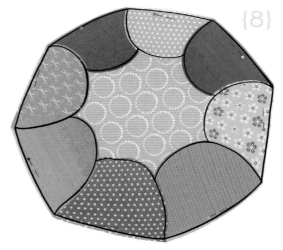

{6} Trim the seam allowance on all the non-stretchy fabrics (you don't need to do this to the stretchy fabrics). Turn the petals right side out. Press the cotton petals.

{8} Place the petals face down on the right side of the flower centre, so that the straight edge of each petal lines up with one side of the flower centre octagon. Pin, then tack the petals in position by hand, 1 cm (⅜ in.) from the raw edges.

{9}

{10}

{9} Place the backing fabric octagon right side down on the flower centre, carefully aligning all the edges, then place the wadding on top. Pin in place, working from the centre outwards, making sure you use plenty of long quilter's pins across the middle of the piece as well as around the edges.

{10} Turn the flower over, so that the wrong side of the main flower centre is facing upwards. Taking a 1-cm (⅜-in.) seam allowance, machine stitch around the edge of the flower centre, removing the pins from underneath as you sew and leaving a 25.5-cm (10-in.) gap in the centre of one of the petals for turning. (You will find it easiest if you leave the gap in one of the cotton fabric petals rather than in one of the petals made from thick or stretchy fabric.)

{11} Turn the play mat right side out through the gap. Press the edges of the gap under in line with the seam on both the back and the front of the play mat and pin in position. Slipstitch the gap closed by hand (see page 7).

{12} Press the flower centre and the cotton petals lightly, taking special care not to iron any synthetic fabrics you have used for your play mat, such as synthetic velour fabric.

Check your fabrics

When making the play mat it is very important to wash all the fabrics before you use them, and to double check that they are all colourfast and non-toxic as babies may put them in their mouths.

Toy boat

This is one of the simplest toys you could ever sew. The secret to making it look lovely lies in your fabric choices. Our version used a plain colour for the hull, with two patterns for the sails and some co-ordinating ribbon. The boat is 30 cm (12 in.) high. You can easily alter the template to make your own boat bigger or smaller – but remember that you might need wider or narrower ribbon for the flags if you do this.

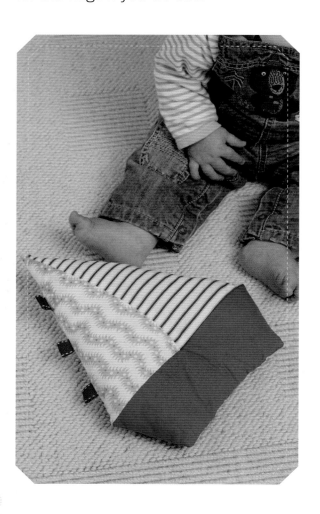

You will need

✂ Two pieces of patterned fabric for the sails, each measuring 31 x 36 cm (12 x 14 in.)

✂ 13 x 31 cm (5 x 12 in.) plain fabric for the hull

✂ 15 cm (6 in.) red ribbon, 15 mm (⅝ in.) wide

✂ Sewing threads to match the fabrics

✂ 45 g (1½ oz) polyester toy filling

✂ One toy rattle insert (you can buy these from shops selling toy-making supplies)

✂ Templates on page 54

✂ Pencil

✂ Paper

✂ Basic sewing kit (see page 4)

Make it personal

For a fun addition to the boat, why not embroider the name of the recipient on the hull – and perhaps add his or her age on the right-hand sail?

How to make the toy boat

{1} Using the templates on page 54, cut out two sail pieces from the first sail fabric and two sail pieces from the second sail fabric, remembering to cut one piece of each fabric with the template the right way up and the other piece with the template face down. Cut out two hull pieces from the plain fabric. Cut the ribbon into three 5-cm (2-in.) lengths.

{2} Place two sail pieces, one of each fabric, right sides together. Taking a 1-cm (⅜-in.) seam allowance, machine stitch them together down the side that forms a right angle to the short edge. Do the same with the remaining two sail pieces. Press the seams open.

{3} With right sides together, aligning the long edge of the hull with the base of the sail, pin one hull piece to one of the double sail pieces. Taking a 1-cm (⅜-in.) seam allowance, machine stitch them together. Press the seam open. Do the same with the other sail and hull piece.

{4} Fold each piece of ribbon in half. Pin the ribbon loops along one side of the sail at 5-cm (2-in.) intervals so that the raw edges of the ribbon line up with the raw edges of the fabric and the loops point inwards.

{5} With right sides together, pin the two boat pieces together, making sure that the seams match. Taking a 1-cm (⅜-in.) seam allowance, machine stitch around the shape using matching threads, changing colour where necessary and leaving a 9-cm (3½-in.) gap along the lower edge of the hull for turning and stuffing.

{6} Snip off the corners of the hull and the point at the top of the sails, taking care not to cut into the stitching. Turn the boat right side out through the gap and press.

{7} Stuff the boat lightly, inserting the rattle into the sail part of the boat. Slipstitch the gap at the lower edge of the hull closed by hand (see page 7).

{8} Work a few hand stitches, one over the other, through both layers of the boat at the point where the lower edges of the sails meet at the centre of the hull to pull it in and create the boat shape.

Templates

Shown at 50% – enlarge by 200% for actual size.

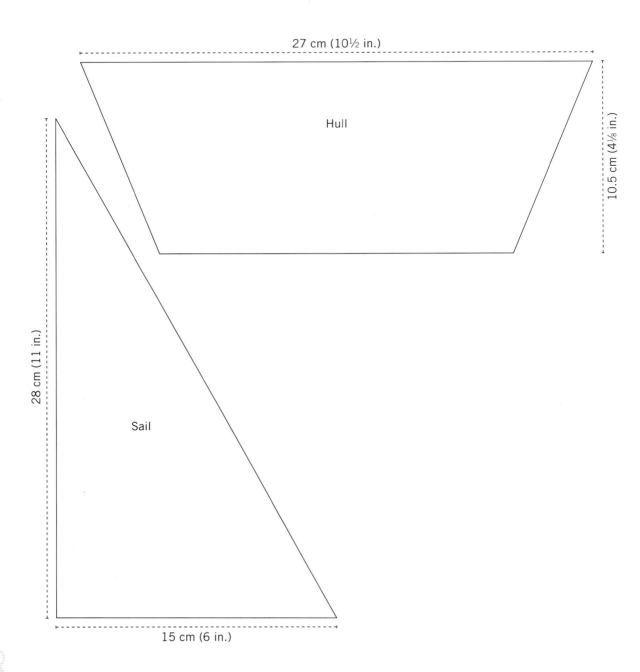

27 cm (10½ in.)

Hull

10.5 cm (4⅛ in.)

28 cm (11 in.)

Sail

15 cm (6 in.)

Antarctic play set

9-12 hrs

Small enough for little hands, and engaging enough to spark any junior imagination, this penguin play set is bound to become a favourite. With a helping hand, the penguins can nestle in their icy cave, dive into the pond to chase for fish… or just generally waddle about. The whole miniature scenario makes a good travel toy, too, as it's light and little enough to carry around and balance on a car or bus seat. Each penguin is about 6 cm (2½ in.) high.

You will need

For each penguin

- Templates below
- Pencil and paper
- 7.5 x 14 cm (3 x 5½ in.) black or dark grey felt
- 4 x 6 cm (1½ x 2½ in.) white felt
- Scrap of orange felt
- White and black sewing threads
- Short length of black embroidery thread
- Small handful of polyester toy filling
- PVA or tacky glue

For the icy landscape

- Two 23 x 33-cm (9 x 13-in.) pieces of white felt
- 9 x 11.5 cm (3½ x 4½ in.) mid-blue felt
- White and blue sewing threads

For the fish

- 5 x 7.5-cm (2 x 3-in.) piece of green felt
- Green sewing thread
- Short length of black embroidery thread
- Water-soluble pen
- Basic sewing kit (see page 4)

Templates
Shown at actual size.

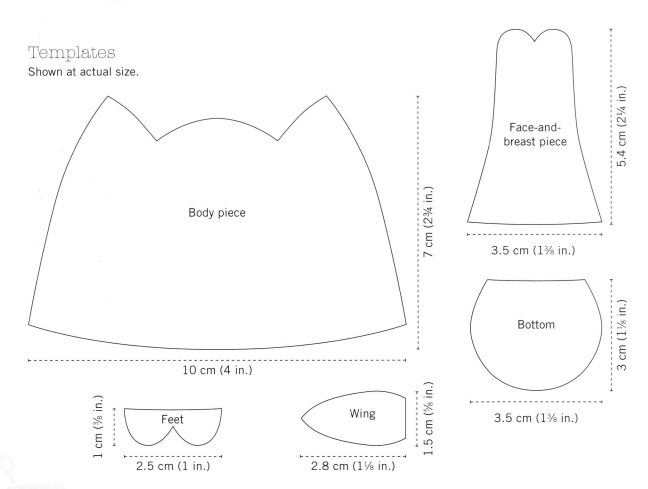

Body piece — 10 cm (4 in.) / 7 cm (2¾ in.)

Face-and-breast piece — 5.4 cm (2¼ in.) / 3.5 cm (1⅜ in.)

Bottom — 3 cm (1⅛ in.) / 3.5 cm (1⅜ in.)

Feet — 1 cm (⅜ in.) / 2.5 cm (1 in.)

Wing — 2.8 cm (1⅛ in.) / 1.5 cm (⅝ in.)

How to make the penguins

{1} Using the templates on page 56, cut out one body piece, two wings and a base from black or grey felt, one face-and-breast piece from white felt, and one foot piece from orange felt.

{2} Place the face-and-breast piece on the centre of the body piece, then work a small running stitch using white thread to sew it in position (see page 7).

{3} Fold the body piece in half so that the face-and-breast piece is on the inside. Using black thread, oversew the back seam. Press the front and back of the head piece together and oversew the top seam.

{4} Turn the penguin right side out. Oversew the tops of the wings in place on the penguin's sides (see page 7).

{5} Embroider two French knots (see the box on page 58) for the eyes, using two strands of black embroidery thread.

{6} Stuff the penguin with polyester toy filling. Oversew the base in place, beginning at the edge of the base of the face-and-breast piece and working around the back of the penguin first. Tuck the foot piece in position at the front and continue oversewing across the base of the face-and-breast piece, catching the foot piece in as you sew.

{7} Cut out a tiny triangle of orange felt for the beak and stick it in place.

Fish

{1} Using the water-soluble pen, draw some small fish shapes on the green felt – but do not cut them out just yet. Using two strands of black embroidery thread, work a French knot on each fish for the eyes.

{2} Place the felt with the fish shapes on top of another piece of green felt and machine stitch around the fish shapes. Cut out the fish shapes, cutting close to the stitching.

Icy landscape

{1} Stack the two pieces of white felt together and use the water-soluble pen to draw curved lines at the two corners on one of the short ends of both rectangles of white felt. Cut along the lines to round off the corners.

{2} Bring the rounded corners of one rectangle towards you, pushing them in towards each other as you do so, to form a small arch about 7.5 cm (3 in.) high, then pin the corners in place approximately halfway down the length of the piece of felt. Oversew along one lower side of the cave using small stitches. Where the edge lifts to form the arch, secure the thread, then work a small running stitch around the edge of the arch (see page 7). When the arch stops, secure the thread, then oversew along the second side of the cave. Remove the pins.

How to make a French knot

Bring your thread out at your starting point. Wind the thread twice round your needle, then take the needle into your fabric just to the side of the starting point. Pull the needle through your fabric, sliding the knot off your needle and onto the fabric as you go.

{4} Work a machine zigzag stitch around the sides and back of the rectangle, then work a curved line of zigzag stitch across the front, following the line just drawn. Now work a line of machine straight stitch along the inside edge of all the zigzag stitching. Trim across the front, just in front of your stitching, taking care not to cut into the stitches.

{5} Flatten the arch temporarily and pin it in place. Oversew the back of the cave to the base rectangle of felt, using small stitches.

{6} Cut out an oval shape measuring approximately 7.5 x 10 cm (3 x 4 in.) from the piece of mid-blue felt for the pond. Pin the pond in place. Zigzag stitch around the outside of the pond in matching thread, then switch your machine to straight stitch to sew along the inside edge of the zigzag stitch.

{3} Place the rectangle with the arch on top of the other rectangle of white felt, so that the front edges meet, and pin them together. Using the water-soluble pen, draw a curved line towards the front of the rectangle. The line does not have to be identical to the one shown, but remember to curve the edges inwards at the sides.

Skinny-eared rabbit

If you want to make a relaxed companion for gentle playtime, check out this Scandi-look bunny. The mix of square body and long, thin ears made it the stand-out favourite with the smaller children who played with it – the ears were perfect for chewing and the body for hugging! The plain linen in our version seems to give it a touch of 'heirloom quality', but you can make it in almost any medium-weight cotton fabric of your choice. The rabbit is about 28 cm (11 in.) high. If you make it for a child under 36 months, please omit the button.

You will need

- ✂ Templates on page 63
- ✂ Pencil
- ✂ Paper
- ✂ 20 x 36 cm (8 x 14 in.) white linen
- ✂ 16.5 x 38 cm (6½ x 15 in.) printed quilting cotton
- ✂ Dark grey stranded embroidery thread
- ✂ Red and white sewing threads
- ✂ 31 cm (12 in.) red ric-rac tape
- ✂ 15-mm (⅝-in.) blue button (optional)
- ✂ 43 g (1½ oz) polyester toy filling
- ✂ Water-soluble pen
- ✂ Basic sewing kit (see page 4)

How to make the skinny-eared rabbit

{1} Using the templates on page 63, cut out two head pieces from the white linen and two body pieces from the printed cotton.

{2} Using the template and the photo on page 60 as a guide, draw the two eyes and the nose on one of the head pieces, using the water-soluble pen. Using all six strands of the grey embroidery thread, hand sew four straight stitches in a cross shape for the nose.

{3} Using three strands of dark grey embroidery thread, hand sew the main part of the eyes in chain stitch (see box). Using the same thread, work the eyelashes in straight stitch.

{4} Pin the ric-rac tape in position 2.5 cm (1 in.) down from the top raw edge of the body piece. Machine stitch it in place down the centre of the tape, using red thread.

{5} Place the two head pieces on the two body pieces, with right sides together and aligning the straight edges. Using white thread and taking a 1-cm (³⁄₈-in.) seam allowance, machine stitch the pieces together along the straight edges. Press the seam towards the body part of the two rabbit shapes.

How to work chain stitch

Bring your needle out at your starting point. Take the needle back into your fabric, just next to the starting point to create a small loop of thread. Bring the needle back up through your fabric a stitch length along and catch the loop with the needle. Pull your thread up gently through the loop until the stitch is firm.

{6} Pin the two rabbit shapes right sides together. Taking a 1-cm (⅜-in.) seam allowance, machine stitch around the outside of the shapes, leaving a 6-cm (2½-in.) gap along one side for turning and stuffing.

{7} Snip into the corners of the rabbit shape at the inner ears, taking care not to cut into the stitching. Turn right side out through the gap and press.

{8} Stuff the rabbit firmly, using the blunt end of a pencil to push the toy filling up to the tips of the ears. Slipstitch the gap at the side closed by hand (see page 7).

{9} Using red thread, sew the button in place at the centre of the ric-rac tape on the front of the rabbit.

Templates

Shown at 40% – enlarge by 250% for actual size.

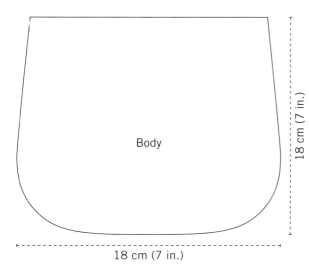

Body

18 cm (7 in.)

18 cm (7 in.)

Eye   Head   Eye

18.5 cm (7¼ in.)

16 cm (6¼ in.)

Fabric garland

1–4 hrs

If your offcuts stash is starting to run over with teeny pieces of gorgeous fabrics, these garlands are a terrific way to use them up. These days fabric garlands aren't reserved for special celebrations – they're a regular ornamental addition to interior decor and look great in children's bedrooms. We made ours in three contrasting cottons, but you could make every flag different if you want a more eclectic feel. And to make a longer garland, just increase the length of the ribbon and measure how many extra shapes it will take to fill it.

You will need

For a 2-m (6 ft 6-in.) garland

✂ Template on page 67

✂ Tracing paper and paper for template

✂ Pencil

✂ Three cotton quilting fabrics in the following sizes:

✂ 24 x 36 cm (9½ x 14 in.) for the slim rectangle garland pieces (fabric A)

✂ 32 x 42 cm (12½ x 16½ in.) for the broad rectangle garland pieces (fabric B)

✂ 45 x 54 cm (17¾ x 21 in.) for the curved garland pieces (fabric C)

✂ Thread to match your fabrics

✂ 2 m (6 ft 6 in.) co-ordinating narrow ribbon

✂ Selection of buttons, lace and embroidery threads

✂ Basic sewing kit (see page 4)

✂ Water-soluble pen

✂ Embroidery needle

✂ Large-eyed blunt sewing needle

How to make the fabric garland

{1} Make templates for the three basic garland shapes. Use the template on page 67 for the curved shape and make your own templates for the rectangles: the slim rectangle pieces measure 8 x 18 cm (3¼ x 7 in.) and the broad rectangles measure 14 x 16 cm (5½ x 6¼ in.). The featured garland consists of four slim rectangles and three each of the other two shapes. Each 'flag' needs two pieces of fabric – so cut out eight slim rectangle shapes from fabric A, six broad rectangles from fabric B and six curved shapes from fabric C.

{2} Pin two of each shape right sides together. On one of the pieces of each 'flag', measure 1 cm (⅜ in.) and 2.5 cm (1 in.) down from the top raw edge and mark these points on each side with a fabric marking pen – these mark where to leave gaps for the ribbon.

{3} Taking a 1-cm (⅜-in.) seam allowance, machine stitch around the edges of each piece, leaving the top edge and the gaps between the two marks open, securing your thread each time you start and stop stitching (see page 7). Clip the curves on the curved pieces and clip the lower corners of the rectangles (see page 7).

{4} Turn all the pieces right side out and press.

{5} Fold in 1 cm (⅜ in.) at the top raw edge of each piece and press. Machine stitch across the top of the flag close to the folded edge, then sew another line of stitching across the flag 1.5 cm (⅝ in.) down from the folded edge to form the casing for the ribbon or cord.

{6} Decorate the pieces using lace, buttons and embroidery thread as shown in the main photograph, stitching through both layers of fabric. The choice of embellishment is yours!

{7} Beginning and ending with a narrow rectangle, arrange the 'flags' in order. Using the large-eyed blunt needle, thread the narrow ribbon through the casing at the top of each piece of bunting.

Template
Shown at 50% – enlarge by 200% for actual size.

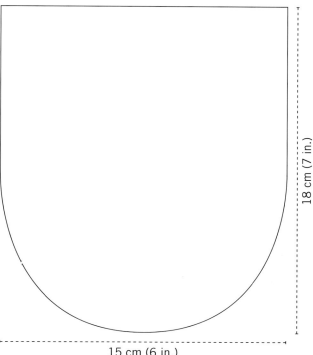

18 cm (7 in.)

15 cm (6 in.)

{6}

{7}

Christmas stockings

If you've had your fill of stockings featuring Santa, Rudolph and their friends, this lively duo offers a suitably festive alternative. The striped stocking ends in a laced trainer, and the spotty one in a neatly buttoned Mary Jane. Both versions were made with contemporary quilting fabrics and lined with soft, cosy fleece. Some pom-pom trim around the top adds the finishing touch. Each stocking is about 46 cm (18 in.) high, so they should be plenty big enough for all those little Christmas treats.

You will need

For each stocking

- 56 x 64 cm (22 x 25 in.) cotton fabric for the main stocking
- 56 x 64 cm (22 x 25 in.) cream fleece fabric for the lining
- Sewing threads to match both fabrics
- 15-cm (6-in.) length of cotton tape, 12 mm (½ in.) wide

For the trainer stocking

- 31-cm (12-in.) square of black felt
- Grey and black sewing thread
- 61-cm (24-in.) black shoelace
- 46 cm (18 in.) green pom-pom trim, 1.5 cm (⅝ in.) wide, and matching thread
- Light-coloured quilter's pencil

For the Mary-Jane shoe stocking

- 31-cm (12-in.) square of red felt
- Red sewing thread
- One 18-mm (¾-in.) white button
- 46 cm (18 in.) red pom-pom trim, 1.5 cm (⅝ in.) wide, and matching thread

- Templates on page 72
- Pencil
- Paper
- Basic sewing kit (see page 4)

How to make the Christmas stocking

{1} Using the templates on page 72, cut out two outer pieces from your main fabric and two lining pieces from fleece for each stocking. For the sneaker stocking, cut out two pieces from black felt using the sneaker template. For the Mary-Jane stocking, cut out two pieces from red felt using the Mary-Jane template, plus a strip of red felt measuring 18 x 2 cm (7 x ¾ in.).

{2} Place one felt shoe piece on the right side of one main outer stocking piece and pin in place. Use your machine to sew around the top edge of the shoe shapes in straight stitch, very close to the edge. For the sneaker, mark a curve for the toe piece with the quilter's pencil, 5 cm (2 in.) in from the edge. Work two lines in straight stitch on either side of the curve, using grey thread. Repeat to create the other side of the stocking.

{3} Place the two outer stocking pieces right sides together, making sure that the shoe parts line up. Pin in place, then machine stitch around the sides and base of the stocking in matching threads, changing the thread colour if necessary and taking a 1-cm (⅜-in.) seam allowance.

{4} Place the two fleece stocking pieces right sides together and machine stitch around the sides and base, taking a 1.5-cm (⅝-in.) seam allowance and leaving a 10-cm (4-in.) gap along the lower edge; you will need this to turn the stocking right side out later on.

{5} Trim all the seam allowances to 6 mm (¼ in.).

{6} Turn the fleece lining right side out and insert it into the outer stocking, which should be wrong side out. Pin the lining and the outer stocking together around the top, making sure that the side seams match. Machine stitch around the top, taking a 1.5-cm (⅝-in.) seam allowance.

{7} Turn the stocking right side out through the gap in the lining. Hand slipstitch the gap in the lining closed (see page 7).

{8} Press the outer stocking. Push the lining down into the outer stocking.

{9} Machine topstitch around the top edge of the stocking, 1 cm (⅜ in.) from the edge (see page 7).

{10} For the Mary-Jane stocking, machine stitch around the strip of red felt for the strap. Stitch it in place at one side, 1 cm (⅜ in.) down from the edge of the shoe. Secure the other side with the button. For the sneaker stocking, make three holes along each side of the sneaker, 1.5 cm (⅝ in.) down from the centre seam, using the point of a small pair of scissors. Thread through the shoelace, using the photograph on page 68 as a guide, and tie it in a bow.

{11} Fold under 1 cm (⅜ in.) at one end of the length of cotton tape. Tuck the other end behind the folded end. Place the loop across the seam on the inside back of the stocking, just down from the top edge, so that the raw edge is concealed. Stitch it in place by working a small square of machine stitching.

{12} Pin the pom-pom trim around the top of the stocking, 1 cm (⅜ in.) down from the top, beginning and ending at the back seam and tucking the raw edges under at each end of the trim. Stitch in place through the outer part of the stocking only, using a hand running stitch and matching thread (see page 7).

Templates

Shown at 25% – enlarge by 400% for actual size.

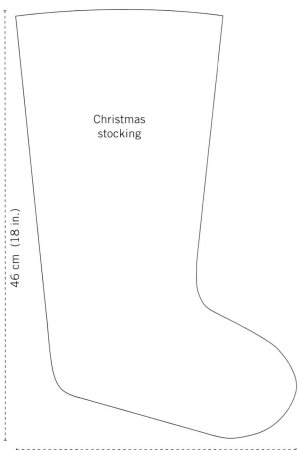

13 cm (5 in.)

Trainer

28 cm (11 in.)

Mary Jane shoe

28 cm (11 in.)

12 cm (4¾ in.)

Christmas stocking

46 cm (18 in.)

28 cm (11 in.)

Tree star

In most homes, the more densely decorated the Christmas tree the better. These tree stars can be hung or usec as tree toppers – add a loop for hanging, or thread some cord through the back to tie the star to the top of your tree. They're simple enough to make a good family project to do with the kids. Choose a special selection of fabrics; they can be a great upcycled use for favourite prints on outgrown or worn-out clothes, which will give them instant nostalgia value. The star measures about 13 cm (5 in.) across.

You will need

- ✂ Template on right
- ✂ Tracing paper and paper to make template
- ✂ Pencil
- ✂ One 20-cm (8-in.) square of each of two contrasting cotton fabrics
- ✂ Cream thread and thread to match your fabrics
- ✂ Mother-of-pearl button, 15 mm (⅝ in.) in diameter
- ✂ 20-cm (8-in.) length of silver cord
- ✂ Small handful of polyester toy filling
- ✂ Basic sewing kit (see page 4)

How to make the tree star

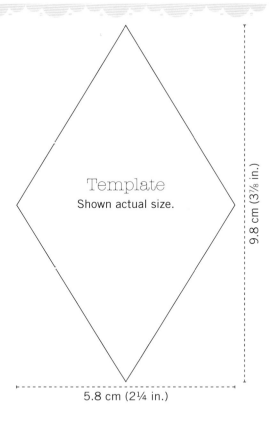

Template
Shown actual size.

9.8 cm (3⅞ in.)

5.8 cm (2¼ in.)

{1} Using the template above, cut out six diamond shapes from each of your two fabrics. You will need three diamond shapes of each fabric to make each side of the star.

{2} Place two diamond shapes in contrasting fabrics right sides together. Taking a 1-cm (⅜-in.) seam allowance, machine stitch the pieces together along one side. Press the seam open.

{3} Place the third diamond face down on the right side of a contrasting diamond. Machine stitch together, starting 1 cm (⅜ in.) from the top edge of the seam near the centre.

{4} Repeat step 3 three more times, so that the six diamonds are all sewn together.

{5} Fold the shape so that the first and last diamond are right sides together. Machine stitch together, again taking a 1-cm (⅜-in.) seam allowance.

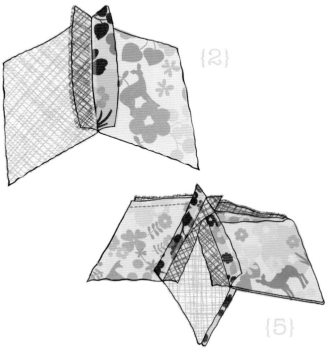

{2}

{5}

{6} Press all the seams open.

{7} Repeat steps 2–4 to make a second star shape. Press under 1 cm (⅜ in.) along the two unsewn sides of the first and last diamonds. (This will form the gap for turning and stuffing once you have sewn the front and back star shapes together.)

{8} Pin the two star shapes right sides together. Machine stitch around the entire outer edge of the star, taking a 1-cm (⅜-in.) seam allowance. Clip the points (see page 7) and clip into the angles between the shapes, taking care not to snip into the stitching.

{9} Turn the star right side out through the gap and press.

{10} For a hanging star (omit this step if your star will be used as a tree topper), thread the length of silver cord through the top of one of the star points from the inside, then thread it back down through the point in the same place. Knot the two ends together. If you are using your star as a tree topper rather than as a hanging decoration, thread the silver cord through the back of the star and use this to tie the star to the top of the tree.

{11} Stuff the star lightly. Hand slipstitch the gap closed (see page 7). Sew the button to the centre front of the star using cream thread, stitching through both sides of the star.

Advent calendar

5–8 hrs

More sophisticated than your average chocolate Advent calendar, and with
a lot more potential for interesting contents, this take on the traditional pre-
Christmas treat is made from twenty-four little felt pockets strung out on a piece of
ribbon. Our numbers have been made using quirky tape-measure print fabric and
self-cover buttons, but you can vary this according to what you can find: try numbers
cut from a real cloth tape measure or counters from an unloved game of bingo.

You will need

✂ Template on page 78

✂ 24 pieces of felt each measuring 6 x 15 cm (2½ x 6 in.); we used four rectangles of felt, each in a different shade and each measuring 20 x 31 cm (8 x 12 in.)

✂ Thread to match all your shades of felt

✂ 24 self-cover buttons, 22 mm (⅞ in.) in diameter

✂ Cotton fabric with tape-measure print; make sure your piece includes all the numbers you need

✂ 3 m (3¼ yd) narrow ribbon or tape

✂ Basic sewing kit (see page 4)

✂ Pair of pliers

✂ Tacky glue

✂ Medium-size safety pin

How to make the advent calender

{1}

{2}

{3}

{1} Cut out all your felt rectangles. Fold down 2 cm (¾ in.) along one short edge of each piece, press in place and then machine stitch close to the raw edge. This will form the casing for your ribbon or tape. The casing will be approximately 1 cm (⅜ in. wide) when finished.

{2} Turn the felt over so that the turned-down edge is on the underside. Turn up the other short edge to 1 cm (⅜ in.) below the folded edge of the casing.

{3} Machine stitch down each side of the pocket, close to the edges.

{4} Using the template below, cut out numbers 1 to 24 from the tape-measure fabric, making sure your numbers are centred on the circle.

Template
Shown at actual size.

3.8 cm (1½ in.)

{5} Using the pliers, remove the button loops from the backs of the buttons.

{6} Using a doubled length of thread, hand sew a line of running stitch round each circle of tape-measure fabric (see page 7). Gather up the stitching, pull the fabric tightly around the button and secure. Then snap on the button backs.

{7} Glue the buttons in place on the felt pockets. To make sure that the glue doesn't seep through and glue the pocket together, tuck bits of paper in the pockets before you glue.

{8} Attach a safety pin to one end of the ribbon, then thread the ribbon through the casing at the top of the felt pockets, making sure you get the numbers in the right order. Fill the pockets with little treats and sit back and wait until 1 December!

Monster
draught buster

5-8 hrs

When the wind starts whistling under the doors on a chilly evening, you know it's time to raid your fabric stash for some co-ordinated cottons to make this friendly monster draught buster. He's a change from the ubiquitous snake or sausage-dog designs and he's fast and straightforward to put together. Measure your door before you start and adjust the pattern up or down for a perfect draught blocker.

You will need

- Templates on page 84
- Tracing paper and paper to make templates
- Pencil
- An assortment of co-ordinating cotton fabrics in the following amounts:
  Two 18 x 21-cm (7 x 8¼-in.) pieces for the head
  One 31 x 42-cm (12 x 16½-in.) piece for the middle body
  One 31 x 27-cm (12 x 10½-in.) piece for the end body
- Small pieces of the fabric you have chosen for the middleof the body, for the ears and the eye base, plus a small piece of the fabric you have chosen for the end of the body for the nose
- One 12 x 15-cm (4¾ x 6-in.) piece of natural linen for the face
- Small piece of cotton wadding for the ears
- One 13 x 22-cm (5 x 8¾-in.) piece of fusible bonding web
- Small black button and a medium-sized mother-of-pearl button for the eyes
- Sewing thread to match your fabrics
- Red sewing thread
- Approx. 150 g (5½ oz) polyester toy filling
- Basic sewing kit (see page 4)
- Water-soluble pen

How to make the monster draught buster

{1} Using the measurements on page 81, cut out two head pieces, one middle and one end body piece from your chosen fabrics. Using the templates on page 84, cut out four ear pieces from the same fabric as the middle body piece and two ear pieces from the wadding.

{2} Place two ear pieces right sides together, with one of the wadding ear pieces on top. Taking a 1-cm (⅜-in.) seam allowance, machine stitch around the curved edge, leaving the straight edge open for turning. Trim the seam allowance, clip the curve (see page 7), turn the ear right side out and press. Repeat for the second ear.

{3} Using fusible bonding web (see page 6) and the face template on page 84, prepare the face appliqué from the natural linen. Cut out and apply it to the centre of the front of one of the head pieces. Machine stitch around the face close to the edge, using matching thread. Make the nose appliqué from the same fabric as the end piece of the body. Press in place and machine stitch around the outer edge. Make the eye base appliqué from the same fabric as the middle body. Press in place and use the straight stitch on your sewing machine to sew a few lines around the outer edge.

{4} Using the water-soluble pen, draw the position of the mouth and left eye on the face. Using red thread and the straight stitch setting on your sewing machine, straight stitch over the mouth line four times. Sew on the buttons for the eyes.

{5} Aligning the raw edges and with the ears pointing downwards, pin the ears in place on the front head piece. Place the back and front head pieces right sides together and use your machine to sew across the top, taking a 1.5-cm (⅝-in.) seam allowance. Press the seam open.

{6} With right sides together, pin and machine stitch the head piece to the middle body piece, taking a 1.5-cm (⅝-in.) seam allowance. Pin and machine stitch the middle body piece to the end body piece, again taking a 1.5-cm (⅝-in.) seam allowance. Press the seams open.

{7} Fold the draught buster in half lengthways, right sides together. Taking a 1.5-cm (⅝-in.) seam allowance, use your machine to sew around the raw edges, leaving a 10-cm (4-in.) gap along the lower edge for turning and stuffing.

{8} To create a flat base for the lower edge of the face and the tail, flatten the lower left corner of the face into a point, so that the seams match at the centre. Sew a straight line across the corner, 2.5 cm (1 in.) down from the pointed edge. Cut off the pointed edge. Repeat for the two corners at the end part of the draught buster.

{9} Turn the draught buster right side out, stuff and slipstitch the gap closed by hand (see page 7).

Templates

Shown at actual size.

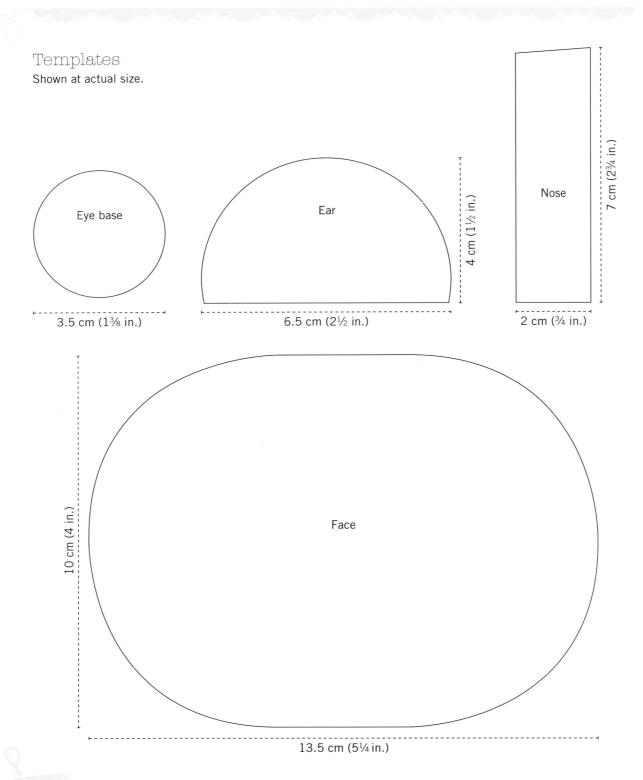

Eye base

3.5 cm (1⅜ in.)

Ear

6.5 cm (2½ in.)

4 cm (1½ in.)

Nose

7 cm (2¾ in.)

2 cm (¾ in.)

Face

10 cm (4 in.)

13.5 cm (5¼ in.)

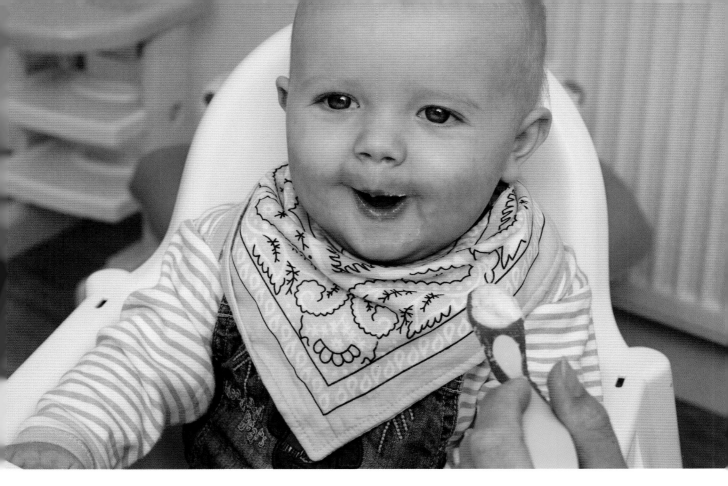

Bandana bib

1-4 hrs

Teddy bears and fluffy chicks are all too common on baby bibs. Tap into some cowboy chic instead, and whip up this version, cut from a genuine bandana, interlined with a piece of brushed cotton, and snapped securely in place at the back. The size given here should fit a baby up to about a year old. For bigger sizes, enlarge the pattern slightly – the bandana will still be large enough.

You will need

✂ Template on page 87

✂ Pencil

✂ One standard-sized cotton bandana about 51 cm (20 in.) square

✂ One triangle of white brushed cotton, the same size as the bandana folded in half diagonally

✂ Sewing thread to match your fabric

✂ Black sewing thread

✂ One 15-mm (⅝-in.) snap fastener

✂ One 18-mm (¾-in.) white button

✂ Basic sewing kit (see page 4)

How to make the baby bib

{1} Wash, dry and press the bandana.

{2} Fold the bandana in half diagonally, so that the fold goes through the points of any square design of the bandana, press along the fold, then open the bandana out flat.

{3} Using the template for half a bandana piece on page 87, cut out two pieces of full bandana, one from each diagonal half, keeping the centre point on the template in line with the diagonal fold.

{3}

28 cm (11 in.) diameter

place on fold of fabric

Template
Shown at 50% – enlarge by 200% for actual size.

22.5 cm (9 in.) diameter

{4}

{4} Place the two bandana pieces right sides together. Lay them on top of the brushed cotton triangle. Pin through all three layers. Machine stitch around the outside edge of the bandana, taking a 1-cm (³⁄₈-in.) seam allowance and leaving a 10-cm (4-in.) gap along the centre of one side for turning. Trim the brushed cotton to the edge of the bandana.

{5} Snip off the front tip of the bib, just to the outside of the seam (this will ensure the front tip of the finished bib is nice and pointy). Turn the bib right side out through the gap and press. Hand slipstitch the gap closed (see page 7).

{6} Topstitch around the entire bib, 6 mm (¼ in.) from the edge (see page 7).

{8}

{7} Sew the base of the snap fastener in place on the right side of one back corner of the bib. Sew the top of the snap fastener in place on a corresponding part on the wrong side of the other back corner.

{8} Using black thread, sew the button in place on the top of the outside of the bandana, over the top part of the snap fastener.

Take-away cup cosy

Everyone should have a personalized cosy: it will keep your coffee warm for longer, stop you burning your hands on a too-hot drink, and also make sure that it doesn't get muddled up with anyone else's. The prototype is designed to fit a cup 11.5 cm (4½ in.) high, but it's easy to create a bespoke fit for the cups at your favourite coffee bar – just follow the simple instructions below.

You will need

- ✂ Template on page 90 (or make your own – see right)
- ✂ Tracing paper and paper for template
- ✂ Pencil
- ✂ 12 x 29 cm (4¾ x 11½ in.) pale pink felt
- ✂ 12 x 29 cm (4¾ x 11½ in.) cotton fabric for the lining, plus a small piece of the same fabric for the mug motif
- ✂ 12 x 29 cm (4¾ x 11½ in.) cotton wadding for the interlining
- ✂ Two 12 x 29-cm (4¾ x 11½-in.) pieces of fusible bonding web, plus a 6-cm (2½-in.) square of bonding web
- ✂ 1 x 8-cm (⅜ x 3¼-in.) strip of sew-on hook-and-loop tape
- ✂ Black sewing thread
- ✂ White sewing thread (if you are using white hook-and-loop tape)
- ✂ Sewing thread to match your fabrics
- ✂ Basic sewing kit (see page 4)
- ✂ Water-soluble pen

Making your own template

To make a template for a cup of your chosen size, wash out an old take-away cup, cut a straight line down the side, remove the base and spread the shape out. Following the curves of the piece, draw a line about 1 cm (⅜ in.) below the rim and 1 cm (⅜ in.) up from the lower edge. Trace this shape onto a piece of paper, then add 1 cm (⅜ in.) to each of the two straight sides.

Template

Shown at 50% – enlarge by 200% for actual size.

5 cm (2 in.)

9 cm (3½ in.)

Mug

4.5 cm (1¾ in.)

place on fold of paper

14 cm (5½ in.)

How to work backstitch

Secure your thread by working a couple of stitches one over the other, then bring your needle out a stitch length along. Take your needle back down into your work at the end of your first stitch to create the back stitch. Then take it out another stitch length along past the previous stitch. Continue in this way till the line is complete.

How to make the take-away cup cosy

{1}

{2}

{1} Using the template above (or the one you have created), draw the cup cosy shape on the felt, but do not cut it out. Mark the centre line as shown.

{2} Using the mug motif template above, the motif fabric and the small square of fusible bonding web, prepare the mug motif appliqué (see page 6).

{3} Cut out the appliqué motif and apply it to the centre of the felt shape.

{4} Using black thread, sew around the mug motif close to the edge. We have used a sewing machine to do this, but if you do not feel confident sewing a small shape, you can hand stitch it instead, using running stitch (see page 7) or backstitch (see above).

{5} Press the bonding web glue side down to one side of the wadding. Peel the backing paper off the bonding web and press the wadding down onto the reverse of the felt (the side without the mug motif).

{6} Press the second rectangle of bonding web glue side down onto the reverse of the rectangle of lining fabric. Peel the backing paper off the bonding web and press the lining fabric down onto the wadding.

{7} Using matching thread, machine stitch around the entire cup cosy shape, just inside the template border. Cut along the template border. Spray or dab with water to remove the water-soluble pen marks.

{8} Oversew the hook side of the hook-and-loop tape onto the left-hand edge of the front of the cosy by hand (see page 7). Oversew the loop side of the hook-and-loop tape onto the right-hand edge of the reverse of the cosy.

Bird coasters

Bring a dash of contemporary style to your coffee table with a flock of silhouette bird coasters. We liked the slightly mismatched look of different colours of felt – but they'd work just as well made all in the same shade. There's a thick layer of wadding sandwiched into the middle of the coasters to make them more substantial and ensure that they are heat resistant. The coasters are super-speedy to make – particularly after you've mastered your first one – and they're an ideal way of using up tiny scraps of favourite fabrics. Each coaster measures just over 10 cm (4 in.) in diameter.

You will need

For each coaster

- ✂ Templates on page 94
- ✂ Tracing paper and paper for template
- ✂ Pencil
- ✂ One 11-cm (4¼-in.) square of coloured felt
- ✂ One 5.5 x 9-cm (2¼ x 3½-in.) piece of charcoal grey felt
- ✂ One 11-cm (4¼-in.) square of cotton fabric to co-ordinate with your felt
- ✂ One 9.5-cm (3¾-in.) square of cotton wadding
- ✂ Two 11-cm (4¼-in.) squares and one 5.5 x 9-cm (2¼ x 3½-in.) piece of fusible bonding web
- ✂ Charcoal grey or black thread
- ✂ Thread to match the coloured felt
- ✂ Basic sewing kit (see page 4)
- ✂ Water-soluble pen

How to make the bird coasters

[1] Using the water-soluble pen and template A below, draw around the shape on your coloured felt but do not cut it out.

[2] Using the small rectangle of bonding web and charcoal felt, prepare the bird appliqué on the charcoal grey felt (see page 6). Cut out the motif and apply it to the coaster in the position shown on the template.

[3] Using charcoal or black thread and a very small running stitch (see page 7), hand stitch around the bird shape.

[4] Place one of the squares of bonding web glue side down on the reverse side of the square of felt with the bird appliqué. Iron in position (see page 6). Cut out the coaster shape.

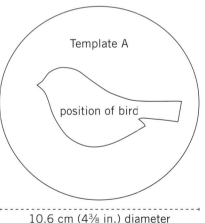

Template A

position of bird

10.6 cm (4⅜ in.) diameter

Templates

Shown at 50% – enlarge by 200% for actual size.

Template B

9 cm (3½ in.) diameter

{5} Using the water-soluble pen and template B on the opposite page, draw around the shape on the piece of wadding and cut out.

{6} Peel the backing paper off the bonding web that is attached to the reverse of the coaster and place the circle of wadding in the centre.

Tip

As a precaution, you can place the paper from the bonding-web square over the coaster before you iron, so that the glue from the bonding web doesn't get on your iron.

{7} Iron the second square of bonding web onto the reverse side of the cotton fabric square. Peel the backing paper off the bonding web and lay the front part of the coaster, together with the wadding, right side up on top. Iron the front of the coaster in place, taking care that the glue from the bonding web on the fabric square does not get onto the iron.

{8} Trim away the excess fabric so that the cotton on the reverse of the coaster matches the felt shape on the front. Using either a machine or hand running stitch and matching thread, sew around the coaster.

Table runner

If you're looking for something classic and beautiful to adorn your table, this Scandinavian-inspired linen runner will meet the need. It's a sophisticated design that's still simple enough to run up in an afternoon. For the leaves, choose a fabric that co-ordinates with your crockery – small prints work best. Our runner is 1.8 m (6 ft) long, but you can adjust the pattern, adding or subtracting pairs of leaves, to make it a customized fit for your own dining table.

You will need

- ✂ 206 x 48 cm (81 x 19 in.) linen fabric
- ✂ One fat quarter (46 x 56 cm/18 x 22 in.) patterned quilting cotton
- ✂ 46 x 56 cm (18 x 22 in.) fusible bonding web
- ✂ 5 m (5½ yd) white ric-rac braid, 1 cm (⅜ in.) wide
- ✂ Seven assorted small to medium white buttons
- ✂ Sewing thread to match the linen fabric and ric-rac braid
- ✂ Green sewing thread
- ✂ Water-soluble pen
- ✂ Template on page 98
- ✂ Pencil
- ✂ Paper
- ✂ Ruler
- ✂ Basic sewing kit (see page 4)

How to make the table runner

{1} Fold under 1.5 cm (⅝ in.) along each long edge of the linen fabric and press. Fold under another 1.5 cm (⅝ in.) and press again. Do the same along the short edges. Tuck in the corners of the short edges and press again. Machine stitch all around the edge of the fabric, close to the inside folded edge, using matching thread.

{2} Sew ric-rac braid around the entire runner, just in from the inside edge. Your stitching should be across the centre of the ric-rac braid and it is easiest to start sewing in the middle of one side rather than at a corner. At the corners, sew to a point just before the end, then, with the needle still in the fabric, raise the machine foot and bring the tape up and over at a right angle, then lower the machine foot again and continue sewing.

{3} Using a water-soluble pen, mark a line down the centre of the runner. Measure 3 cm (1¼ in.) from one end of the centre line and make a mark. This will be the start of the stalk. Measure 13 cm (5 in.) from the first mark to make a second mark. This will be where the first pair of leaves will be attached to the stalk. Measure 23 cm (9 in.) from this mark and make another mark for the placement of the second pair of leaves. Do this five times more, spacing the marks 23 cm (9 in.) apart, to mark where five more pairs of leaves will be placed. Measure 16 cm (6¼ in.) from the last mark to make an eighth and final mark for the position of the base of a single leaf.

Template
Shown at 50% – enlarge by 200% for actual size.

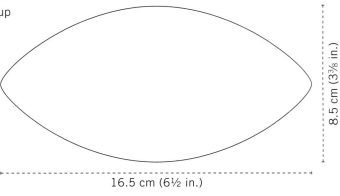

8.5 cm (3⅜ in.)

16.5 cm (6½ in.)

{4} Fold the short edge of a standard-sized sheet of paper to one of its long edges to make a 45-degree angle. By placing the paper along the central line and drawing along the angle, make pairs of 16 cm (6¼ in.) lines at 45-degree angles up and away from the stalk at each of the seven marks you made for the pairs of leaves.

{6} Following the instructions on page 6, iron the leaves along the centre line so that the tops and bottoms of the leaves are on the 45-degree lines and there is a slight gap between the bases of the leaves. The base of the top leaf should be on the top mark. Using green thread and starting at the bottom of the stalk, machine straight stitch up to the first pair of leaves. Stitch around the pair of leaves. Repeat the stitching up the stalk and around each pair of leaves until you reach the final leaf. Stitch around the top leaf, then stitch up and down the stalk a couple more times before finishing.

{5} Create your copy of the template on page 98. Press the bonding web onto the wrong side of the quilting fabric and draw around the template to make 15 leaf appliqués (see page 6).

{7} Stitch a button in place at the base of each pair of leaves and at the bottom of the top leaf.

Apron

One-size-fits-all aprons tend, exasperatingly, not to fit anyone very well –
but this model is an exception. Now everyone can cut a sartorial dash in the
kitchen. The head loop and waist ties are a continuous length of tape, threaded
through channels on the sides of the apron bib, so you can adjust the whole thing
to fit anyone from a biggish child to a large adult. Add an appliqué of your choice
and you have a fully personalized product that you'll enjoy wearing. If you feel like
it, you could even make a set – one for each member of the family – to encourage
cooperative cooking efforts...

You will need

- ✂ Templates on page 105
- ✂ Tracing paper and paper for templates
- ✂ Pencil
- ✂ 90 cm (35½ in.) printed linen fabric at least 115 cm (45 in.) wide
- ✂ 3 m (3¼ yd) linen tape, 2.5 cm (1 in.) wide
- ✂ 13 x 23 cm (5 x 9 in.) cotton fabric for the appliqué
- ✂ 13 x 23 cm (5 x 9 in.) fusible bonding web
- ✂ Thread to match your fabric
- ✂ White button, 20 mm (¾ in.) in diameter
- ✂ Basic sewing kit (see page 4)
- ✂ Water-soluble pen
- ✂ Large safety pin for threading the ties

How to make the apron

{1} Following the instructions on page 6, make the templates (see page 105). Use the templates to cut out your apron fabric: you will need one main piece and two facings. Cut out one facing using your template the right way up and one using your template face down.

{2} Lay the main apron piece right side up on your work surface, with one of the facings right side down on top, aligning the raw edges. Pin together and machine stitch, taking a 1-cm (⅜-in.) seam allowance. Sew the other facing on in the same way. Clip the curves (see page 7) and press the seams open.

{3} If your fabric is prone to fraying, zigzag stitch along the raw edges of the facings. Then fold under 1 cm (⅜ in.) along these edges. Press in place.

{4} Fold under 1 cm (⅜ in.) along the top edge of the apron, including the facings, and press. Fold under another 1 cm (⅜ in.) and press again. Machine stitch close to the lower folded edge.

{5} Fold under 1 cm (⅜ in.) along both sides of the apron, including the facings, and press. Fold under another 1 cm (⅜ in.) and press again. Machine stitch close to the inner folded edge.

{6} Fold the facings in and press. Pin in place, then machine stitch close to the inside folded edge along the long edges of the facings to form casings for the apron straps.

{7} Fold up 1 cm (⅜ in.) along the lower edge of the apron and press. Fold up 1.5 cm (⅝ in.) and press again. Machine stitch close to the upper folded edge.

{8} Cut out a piece of fabric measuring 41 x 28 cm (16 x 11 in.) for the pocket. Turn under 1 cm (⅜ in.) along the lower edge and press. Turn under another 1 cm (⅜ in.) and press again. Machine stitch close to the top of the folded edge. Repeat this process along the two sides.

{9} Turn under 1 cm (⅜ in.) along the top edge of the pocket and press. Turn under another 4 cm (1½ in.) and press again. Machine stitch close to the lower folded edge.

{10} Using the printed cotton and bonding web, prepare the fish appliqué motif (see page 6). Cut out the motif and apply it to the pocket, centred on the pocket width and with the lower edge of the fish about 6 cm (2½ in.) up from the lower edge of the pocket.

{11} Pin the pocket in position in the centre of the apron, 15 cm (6 in.) up from the bottom of the apron. Machine stitch around the sides and lower edge of the pocket, close to the edge, reverse stitching at the top edges to make sure it is secure (see page 7).

{12} Sew on the button for the fish's eye.

{13} Attach a safety pin to one end of the linen tape, then thread the tape up through the lower edge of one of the side casings and out through the top. Then thread the tape back down through the top of the second side casing and out through the lower edge.

{14} Fold under 2.5 cm (1 in.) at each end of the tape and press. Fold under another 2.5 cm (1 in.) and press again. Sew around the tape in a square shape. Adjust the tape to fit.

Templates

Shown at 20% – enlarge by
500% for actual size.

Cut curve here

Cut curve here

Place this edge along the fold of the paper

22 cm (8¾ in.)

5.5 cm
(2³⁄₁₆ in.)

92 cm (36 in.)

61 cm (24 in.)

66 cm (26 in.)

Sarong

Is it a skirt? Is it a dress? Is it a beach wrap? It's all three, of course, because it's a sarong. Made from a simple piece of hemmed fabric, it's hardly surprising that the sarong is one of the most popular items of clothing worldwide. I added a border to ours because I thought it would be a great way to make a small-but-beautiful remnant of Liberty Tana lawn work a lot harder, and I made a neat travel bag to pop it in, too. For the simplest version possible, though, you could just hem the right-sized piece of fabric and be ready to go!

You will need

For the sarong

- ✕ 97 x 142 cm (38 x 56 in.) cream cotton or cotton mix fabric
- ✕ 70 x 142 cm (28 x 56 in.) printed cotton lawn
- ✕ Stranded pink embroidery thread to co-ordinate with the cotton lawn
- ✕ Cream sewing thread

For the travel bag

- ✕ Template on page 110
- ✕ Tracing paper and paper for template
- ✕ Pencil
- ✕ Two 20 x 31-cm (8 x 12-in.) pieces of cream cotton or cotton mix fabric
- ✕ Scrap of printed cotton lawn left over from making the sarong
- ✕ Small piece of bonding web
- ✕ 120 cm (47 in.) pale blue ribbon, 6 mm (¼ in.) wide

- ✕ Cream sewing thread
- ✕ Basic sewing kit (see page 4)
- ✕ Water-soluble pen
- ✕ Small safety pin for threading the ribbon of the travel bag

How to make the sarong

{1} Cut your printed cotton lawn lengthways into four equal strips. With right sides together, aligning the raw edges, pin one cotton lawn strip to one long side of the main piece. Machine stitch together, taking a 1-cm (⅜-in.) seam allowance. Repeat for the other long side. Press the seams towards the printed cotton lawn strips.

{3} Fold under 1.5 cm (⅝ in.) on one short edge of the third border piece and press. With right sides together, aligning the long raw edges, pin the border piece to a short side of the main piece. Trim the border piece so that it extends 1.5 cm (⅝ in.) beyond the edge of the main piece. Fold the extending edge under to align with the main piece and press.

{4} Machine stitch the border in place, taking a 1-cm (⅜-in.) seam allowance, and press the seam towards the cotton lawn fabric. Repeat steps 3 and 4 to make the border for the second short side.

{2} Fold under 1 cm (⅜ in.) along the raw edge of one of the border pieces and press. Fold the border over so that the folded edge overlaps the seam by just under 2 mm (¹⁄₁₆ in.). Pin on the right side, then machine stitch down this line. Repeat for the other border.

{5} Fold under 1 cm (⅜ in.) along the raw edge of one of the short borders and press. Fold the border over so that the folded edge overlaps the seam by just under 2 mm (¹⁄₁₆ in.). Pin on the right side, then machine stitch down this line. Repeat for the other border.

{6} Slipstitch the gaps at the corners closed by hand (see page 7).

Wear it in all sorts of ways

For loads of ideas on the different ways you can wear your sarong, just type 'how to wear a sarong' into your favourite search engine. After checking out the results, you certainly won't be short of ideas!

{7} Using the water-soluble pen, draw a line all around the main cream part of the sarong, just over 6 mm (¼ in) from the seam line between the main fabric and the border pieces. Using three strands of pink embroidery thread, work over this line in a medium-length hand running stitch (see page 7).

Travel bag

{1} Using your sewing machine, zigzag stitch around all four sides of the two cream rectangles.

{2} Using the template below, the bonding web and the scrap of border fabric, prepare the heart appliqué motif (see page 6). Cut out the appliqué motif and apply it to the centre of one of the pieces of cream fabric, 7 cm (2¾ in.) up from one of the short edges. Straight stitch around the edge of the appliqué, using cream thread.

{3} Place the two cream rectangles right sides together. Using the water-soluble pen, make marks 2 cm (¾ in.) and 4.5 cm (1¾ in.) down from the top edge on both sides of the rectangles. Machine stitch around the sides and base of the bag, taking a 1-cm (⅜-in.) seam allowance and leaving gaps between the two marks on each side. Press the side seams open.

{4} Turn down 1 cm (⅜ in.) all the way around the top edge and press. Then fold down again so that the top mark aligns with the bottom mark and press. Machine stitch around the top edge close to the lower folded edge. Turn the bag right side out and press.

{5} Divide the ribbon into two equal lengths. Attach a small safety pin to one end of one length, then feed the ribbon through the channel all the way around from the hole in one of the side seams and knot the ends together. Thread the other piece of ribbon all the way around from the other side and, again, knot the ends together.

Template
Shown at 50% – enlarge by 200% for actual size.

10 cm (4 in.)

9.5 cm (3¾ in.)

Felt sandals

5–8 hrs

Creating your own footwear can be easier than it sounds – and this way
of making a good warm pair of indoor sandals is very speedy indeed. You use
an existing pair of sandals or flipflops as a pattern, so a great fit is a given, and
they're crafted from very thick felt (easily available online). The basic shoe is
created from a single piece: you cut the straps as part of the main shoe and stitch
them together at the top. And you can make them in any size, from small kid to
large adult, and embellish (or not) to suit. Read on to see just how simple it is…

You will need

- Pair of simple thong sandals or similar to use as a template
- Template on page 113
- Tracing paper and paper for template
- Pencil
- Two 31-cm (12-in.) squares of fusible bonding web
- One 31-cm (12-in.) square of grey spotted cotton fabric
- 43 x 58 cm (17 x 23 in.) pale grey felt, approx. 4 mm (⅛ in.) thick
- Small piece of standard-sized green felt
- Two flower-shaped pink buttons
- Grey and green sewing threads
- Basic sewing kit (see page 4)
- Water-soluble pen

How to make the felt sandals

{1} Using your existing sandals as a template, draw around the right and left sandals on one of the pieces of bonding web. Place the bonding web glue side down on the reverse of the grey spotted cotton fabric, iron in place and cut out the sandal linings.

{2} Peel off the backing paper from the linings and place them glue side down on the grey felt. Press in place. Cut your felt to match the linings to create the sandal insoles.

{3} You will need to make a template for the base and the straps of each sandal. Put one of your sandals on a piece of brown paper and draw around it. Add a 5 x 9 cm (2 x 3½in.) rectangle on each side for the straps in the place where you want the strap to come across your foot. Use these templates to cut two outer sandal pieces from the pale grey felt.

{4} Machine stitch around the strap part of the outer sandal pieces in grey thread, 6 mm (¼ in.) from the edges, making sure that your stitching begins and ends in the centre of the curves.

{5} Place the insole pieces right side up on the top of your main sandal shapes and pin in place. Machine stitch around the insole in grey thread, 6 mm (¼ in.) from the edge.

{6} Use the leaf template below and the water-soluble pen to create the outlines of four leaves on the green felt. Machine stitch around the edges of the shapes in green thread, beginning and ending your stitching at one end of the leaves. Sew two lines down the centre of each leaf, ending your stitching at the same end of the leaves. Cut around the leaves carefully, leaving your thread tails intact.

{7} Overlap the straps of the sandals so that the inside strap is uppermost and pin in place. Stitch the leaves and the button in place, catching the two straps of the sandal together as you do so to secure them.

Template
Shown at actual size.

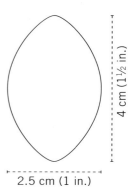

4 cm (1½ in.)

2.5 cm (1 in.)

Baby shoes

These are the easiest baby shoes you could ever make. There are just
two pattern pieces and no fiddly elastic or fastenings. The fleece lining helps
them to stay put on little feet as well as keeping your baby cosy on cool days.
The shoe template is supplied in two sizes, so you can make the shoes for babies
up to three months or from three to six months.

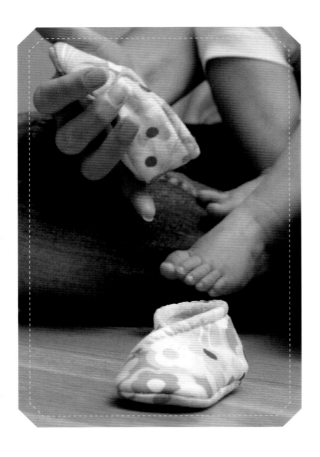

You will need

- ✂ Templates on page 116
- ✂ Pencil
- ✂ Paper
- ✂ 31 x 46 cm (12 x 18 in.) patterned cotton fabric
- ✂ 31 x 46 cm (12 x 18 in.) fleece in a colour that is co-ordinated with the cotton fabric
- ✂ Matching sewing thread
- ✂ Basic sewing kit (see page 4)

How to make the baby shoes

{1} Pin your copies of the templates below to the fabric and cut out two top pieces and two sole pieces from your patterned cotton fabric, remembering to cut one sole piece with the template face up and the other with it face down. Cut out two top pieces and two rectangles that are slightly bigger than the sole pieces from the fleece.

{2} With wrong sides together, pin the outer fabric sole pieces to the fleece rectangles. Machine stitch around the outer sole pieces, very close to the edge. Trim the fleece rectangles to the same size as the outer fabric soles.

Template

Shown at 50% – enlarge by 200% for actual size.

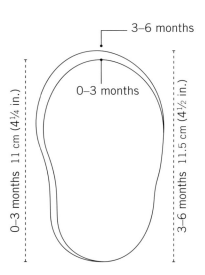

3–6 months

0–3 months

0–3 months 11 cm (4¼ in.)

3–6 months 11.5 cm (4½ in.)

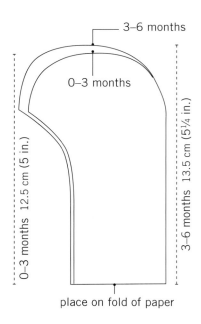

3–6 months

0–3 months

0–3 months 12.5 cm (5 in.)

3–6 months 13.5 cm (5¼ in.)

place on fold of paper

{3} Place one outer and one fleece top piece right sides together. Machine stitch along the top edge, taking a 6-mm (¼-in.) seam allowance. Turn right side out and press lightly on the outer fabric. Topstitch along the top edge just over 6 mm (¼ in.) from the edge.

{4} Place the sole and top piece right sides together and pin the centre of the top piece to the centre of the back of the heel.

{5} Starting from the centre of the heel, pin one side of the top piece around the outer side of the shoe, across the front and then down the first part of the inner side. Machine stitch in place, taking a 6-mm (¼-in.) seam allowance.

{6} Pin the other side of the top piece in position and stitch in place, again taking a 6-mm (¼-in.) seam allowance. Work a zigzag stitch around the seam allowance.

{7} Turn the shoe right side out. Repeat steps 3–7 to make the second shoe, remembering that it will be a mirror image of the shoe you have just made.

Lavender underwear sachet

A cute update on the classic lavender bag, to keep your clothes drawers sweet smelling (and moth free). You can't have too many (and they make good stocking fillers, too), so mix up different prints and trims and use the patterns to appliqué them with knickers or underpants in a range of styles and various colours and textures. Lavender sachets last much longer when they're lavishly filled, so try to lay your hands on a generous supply of lavender flowers. The sachets measure about 5 x 8 cm (2 x 3¼ in.).

You will need

For each lavender sachet

✂ Templates on page 121

✂ Tracing paper and paper for template

✂ Pencil

✂ Two rectangles of natural linen, each measuring 11.5 x 15 cm (4½ x 6 in.)

✂ 7 x 10 cm (2¾ x 4 in.) printed cotton

✂ 7 x 10 cm (2¾ x 4 in.) fusible bonding web

✂ Thread to match your natural linen

✂ Thread to contrast with your printed cotton

✂ Small ready-made white bow and a mother-of-pearl button 6 mm (¼ in.) in diameter (for the girl's pants only)

✂ Tiny white button (for the boy's boxer shorts only)

✂ 3 tablespoons of dried lavender flowers

✂ Basic sewing kit (see page 4)

✂ Teaspoon

How to make the lavender underwear sachets

{1} Using your chosen template on page 121, the printed cotton and the bonding web, prepare your underwear appliqué motif (see page 6) and cut it out.

{4} Place the two rectangles of linen right sides together and machine stitch around the outside, taking a 1-cm (3/8-in.) seam allowance and leaving a 5-cm (2-in.) gap in one side for turning.

{2} Peel off the backing paper and press the appliqué onto the centre of the right side of one of the linen rectangles. Machine stitch around the appliqué in contrasting thread, using the template and photos on pages 118–119 as a guide.

{3} Referring to the photos on pages 118–119, decorate the front of the sachet with a tiny ribbon bow or button.

{5} Clip the corners of the sachet (see page 7), turn it right side out through the gap in the side and press.

{6} Using a teaspoon, fill the sachet with lavender flowers. Slipstitch the gap closed by hand (see page 7).

Templates

Shown at actual size.

8.5 cm (3⅜ in.)

5 cm (2 in.)

8 cm (3¼ in.)

5.5 cm (2³⁄₁₆ in.)

8.3 cm (3¼ in.)

5.5 cm (2³⁄₁₆ in.)

Wrap skirt

Most home sewers have, at one time or another, seen some great fabric, thought about sewing a skirt... and then changed their mind. It's the fatal combination of darts, a tricky zip and a fiddly waistband that does it. So here is a pattern for a skirt that doesn't require any of those things, cut on the bias for extra swing, and flattering to a wide range of shapes and sizes. It's comfortable to wear, too, so once you've made one, you'll want to make several. Vary them with different prints, textures and trimmings.

Sizing

The skirt will fit UK sizes 8–14 (US 6–12), depending on where you sew the second tie (this will become clear a bit later). It is 55 cm (21½ in.) long, which means it will be about knee length on an average-height woman when worn 5 cm (2 in.) or so below the natural waistline. If you want a larger or smaller size, just make the pieces a little wider or narrower. This isn't couture tailoring! You could also easily make it a bit shorter or longer by extending the shape at the bottom. Remember that if you make it longer you will need more fabric and extra trimming.

You will need

- ✂ Templates on page 127
- ✂ Tracing paper and paper for templates
- ✂ Pencil
- ✂ 1.5 m (60 in.) fabric that is at least 111 cm (44 in.) wide; you will need more if the pattern on your fabric has a repeat of more than a few centimetres
- ✂ 2.2 m (2½ yd) orange ric-rac tape, 2.5 cm (1 in.) wide
- ✂ Thread to match fabric and ric-rac tape
- ✂ Small snap fastener
- ✂ Basic sewing kit (see page 4)

How to make the wrap skirt

{1} Following the instructions on page 6, make your templates for the skirt pieces.

{2} Cut out all the skirt and facing pieces on the bias (see page 6). Cut one piece for the skirt back in the fabric and the facing by folding back the seam allowance where marked on the templates and placing the folded edge of the templates on the fold of your fabric. Unfold the seam allowance and cut two pieces each for the skirt front in the fabric and the facing. If your fabric has an obvious pattern direction like ours, try to match the design where possible, so that it will face the same way on the finished skirt. Cut out two bias strips, each measuring 4 x 55 cm (1½ x 21½ in.) for the ties.

{3} Fold under 6 mm (¼ in.) along one of the short edges of each tie and press. Fold under 6 mm (¼ in.) along the two long edges and press. Fold the piece in half lengthways, press again, then machine stitch the folded short edge and the long edges together, very close to the edge.

{4} Work a line of zigzag stitching down the sides of the three main fabric pieces of the skirt.

{5} With right sides together, aligning the raw edges, place one front fabric piece on the back fabric piece. Pin in place, then machine stitch the seam, taking a 1-cm (⅜-in.) seam allowance. Sew the other front fabric piece to the other side of the skirt in the same way. Press the seams open.

{6} Join the three pieces of the facing together in the same way, taking 1-cm (⅜-in.) seam allowances. Press the seams open.

{7} With right sides together, matching the seams and aligning the top raw edges, place the facing on the skirt. Machine stitch the facing to the skirt along the entire top edge, taking a 1-cm (⅜-in.) seam allowance. Press the seam open.

{8} Fold under 1 cm (⅜ in.) along the sides of the skirt piece, including the facing, and press. Fold in another 1 cm (⅜ in.) and press again. Machine stitch close to the folded edges.

{9} Fold the raw top edge of the facing down by 1 cm (⅜ in.) and press. Fold the facing down along the seam where it meets the main part of the skirt and press. Pin in place and then machine stitch close to the lower edge of the facing.

{10} With the wrong side of the skirt facing you, insert the first 1.5 cm (½ in.) of the raw edge of one of the ties into the top part of the gap at the top side edge of the skirt. Work two lines of stitching over the stitching already there to secure the tie.

{11} Slipstitch the tie to the edges of the skirt (see page 7). Slipstitch the gap in the right-hand side of the skirt closed.

{12} Try the skirt on for fit to decide where you want to sew the second tie. Lay the tie on the waist of the skirt so that the raw edge is on the left. Machine stitch a double line of stitching 1 cm (⅜ in.) from the raw edge. Move the main part of the tie from the right to the left, covering the raw edge, and sew another double line of stitching to secure the tie.

{13} Fold up 1 cm (⅜ in.) along the lower edge of the skirt and press. Fold up another 1.5 cm (½ in.) and press again. Machine stitch close to the top folded edge.

{14} Pin the ric-rac tape in place round the lower edge of the skirt, 2.5 cm (1 in.) or so from the lower edge. To make your trimming look really neat, turn over the raw edges of the ric-rac and tuck it around the sides of the skirt before you sew it on. Machine stitch a line through the centre of the ric-rac.

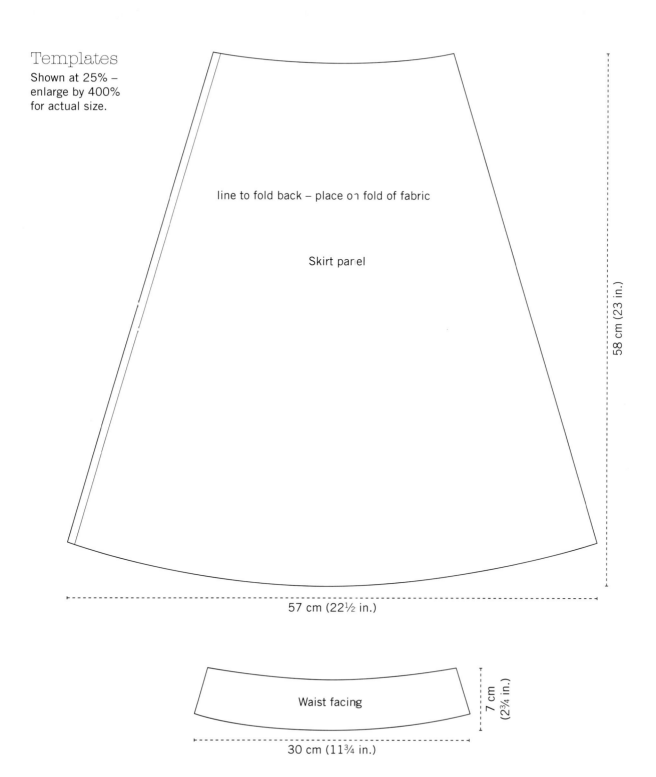

Templates

Shown at 25% – enlarge by 400% for actual size.

line to fold back – place on fold of fabric

Skirt panel

58 cm (23 in.)

57 cm (22½ in.)

Waist facing

7 cm (2¾ in.)

30 cm (11¾ in.)

Pompom-trimmed baby jacket

Every baby needs a jacket or two to look their best when they're out and about. This wrap-style baby jacket is made from a pretty quilting fabric, lined with fleece – and is an absolute cinch to make. I added in a mini pom-pom trim, but you could leave it plain if you prefer, which would make the jacket even quicker to sew. The garment is designed to fit an average-size baby of six months, but you can size the pattern up or down a bit to fit a slightly bigger or smaller baby.

You will need

✂ Templates on page 133

✂ Pencil

✂ Paper

✂ 64 x 107 cm (25 x 42 in.) quilting cotton fabric

✂ 64 x 107 cm (25 x 42 in.) cream fleece fabric

✂ Sewing thread to match your fabrics

✂ 180 cm (2 yd) co-ordinating mini pom-pom trim

✂ Two 12-mm (½-in.) snap fasteners

✂ Stitch ripper

✂ Basic sewing kit (see page 4)

How to make the
pompom-trimmed baby jacket

{1} Using the templates on page 133, cut out a
back piece and a right and left front piece from
both your main fabric and the fleece lining.
When cutting the front pieces, remember to cut
out one piece using the pattern the right way up
and one using it face down. Cut the sleeves on
both the front and back pieces of the fleece
lining 2 cm (¾ in.) shorter than the sleeves on
the main jacket pieces.

A word about fleece

Fleece has a 'nap' – which means that the
fibres lie down in one direction. Before cutting
your fleece, check that the nap flows down the
length of the jacket. Before sewing, check the
right side and wrong side of your fleece – they
are similar and it is quite easy to get them the
wrong way round.

{2} With right sides together, place one of the front
pieces of the main fabric on the corresponding part
of the back piece and pin in place. Taking a 1-cm
(⅜-in.) seam allowance, machine stitch along the top
of the sleeve and then stitch along the lower sleeve
and the side. Clip the curves (see page 7) and press
the seams open. Repeat for the other side.

{3} Make the fleece lining in exactly the same way as the outer jacket, but do not clip the curves or press the seams open. Trim the seam allowance to approximately 6 mm (¼ in.). Turn right side out.

{4} Turn the outer jacket right side out and press. Tack the pom-pom trim to the front and neck section of the main jacket piece along the line on the trimming where you are going to sew your seam, 1 cm (⅜ in.) in from the raw edge and the pom-poms facing inwards. Do the same along the lower edge of the jacket. Turn the jacket inside out.

{5} Insert the lining into the outer part of the jacket, right sides together, and pin them together along the neck edge, matching the shoulder seams. Then pin along the lower edge, matching the side seams. Use your machine to sew along the tacking line where you attached the pom-pom trim, stitching 1 cm (⅜ in.) in from the raw edge, then remove the tacked stitches with a stitch ripper.

{6} With the wrong side of the outer jacket facing you, machine stitch along the short front edge on the left front if your jacket is for a girl, or on the short front edge on the right front if your jacket is for a boy, taking a 1-cm (⅜-in.) seam allowance. On the opposite side, sew the seam, using the same seam allowance, but leaving a gap of 5 cm (2 in.) in the middle of the seam. You will use the gap in the middle of this side to turn your jacket right side out.

{7} Turn the jacket right side out through the gap. Slipstitch the gap closed (see page 7). Push the fleece sleeve linings into the main sleeves. Press the jacket lightly on the outer part only.

{8} Fold under 1 cm (⅜ in.) to the wrong side around the cuffs of the sleeves and press. Fold under another 1 cm (⅜ in.) and press again. Insert the fleece sleeve lining under the folded edge and pin in place. Machine stitch close to the folded edge.

{9} Fold the appropriate side of the front over the other front piece, and sew the snap fasteners in place to secure the front of the jacket.

Templates

Shown at 25% – enlarge by 400% for actual size.

31 cm (12 in.)

32 cm (12½ in.)

31 cm (12 in.)

47 cm (18½ in.)

Strapped sundress

A cool, floaty cotton sundress is an ideal pick on a hot summer's day.
This one is made from a single rectangle of fabric – with the almost magical addition of some stretchy thread called shirring elastic, which gathers your fabric as you sew. This dress has narrow shoulder straps made from the same fabric, but you could use lengths of ribbon instead, which would make it even simpler to sew. The instructions here are for a dress to fit a five-year-old girl, but you can adjust the size up or down to fit your child.

Fabric quantities

To work out how much fabric you will need, you will need to take two measurements. First, measure around the child's chest. Then measure from the armpit to the point at which you would like the dress to end. Cut out a piece of fabric twice as wide as the chest measurement and 6 cm (2½ in.) longer than the desired finished length. For my dress, designed to fit an average size five-year-old girl, I used a rectangle of fabric measuring 66 cm (26 in.) wide by 71 cm (28 in.) long. If your fabric has an obvious direction, remember that the pattern should run down the length of the fabric. For the straps, cut four pieces of fabric, each measuring 4 x 38 cm (1½ x 15 in.).

You will need

- ✂ Lightweight cotton for the main dress, plus 15 x 38 cm (6 x 15 in.) for the straps (see box)
- ✂ Thread to match your fabric
- ✂ Shirring elastic (elastic thread); this is normally available only in black or white – choose white for a light-coloured fabric and black for a darker fabric
- ✂ Elastic, long enough to go round the child's chest and 6 mm (¼ in.) wide
- ✂ Small safety pin
- ✂ Basic sewing kit (see page 4)

How to make the strapped sundress

{1} Using your sewing machine, zigzag stitch close to the raw edge of the two long side edges of the rectangle; these are the edges that will form the back seam.

{2} Fold under 1.5 cm (⅝ in.) along the top edge and press. Fold under another 1.5 cm (⅝ in.) and press again. Machine stitch just over 6 mm (¼ in.) away from the top folded edge to form the casing. (This will allow you to thread the 6 mm/¼-in wide elastic through the casing to make sure that the dress fits snugly.)

{3} Wind the shirring elastic tightly around your bobbin by hand (if you don't wind it sufficiently tight, you won't get the right effect so it's a good idea to practise with some spare elastic and fabric first). Keep your matching top thread for the stitching on the right side of your fabric.

{4} With the right side of your fabric facing you, sew the first row of shirring 1.5 cm (⅝ in.) below the stitching on your casing. Sew another nine rows of shirring, each 1.5 cm (⅝ in.) apart. Keep an eye on your bobbin, as you will probably need to rewind it with shirring elastic a few times during this process. If your dress is for a very small child, reduce the number of rows here. If your dress is for a larger child, add two or three more rows.

{5} Attach a small safety pin to one end of the elastic, then thread it through the top casing of the dress and secure with a few hand stitches at each end (see page 7). Remove the safety pin.

{6} With right sides together, aligning the zigzagged edges, fold the dress in half widthways. Pin and then machine stitch along the back seam, taking a 1-cm (⅜-in.) seam allowance. Press the seam open.

{7} For the hem, turn up 1 cm (⅜ in.) along the lower edge and press. Then turn up 2 cm (¾ in.) and press again. Machine stitch close to the folded edge.

{8} For the straps, fold under 6 mm (¼ in.) along both short edges of one piece and press. Fold the piece in half lengthways and press. Open the piece out again, fold the two outer edges to the centre crease and press. Fold the pieces in half lengthways again, making sure the long folded edges line up, and press again. Machine stitch along the long edges, close to the folded edges, and sew along one of the shorter edges. Make the other three straps in the same way.

{9} To work out the best position for the straps, try the dress on the child first and mark the position. Hand stitch the unstitched end of the straps to the inside of the dress, along the lower edge of the casing. On the right side of the dress, hand slipstitch the strap in place along the top edge of the casing (see page 7).

Pyjama bottoms

Nothing signals the beginning of the perfect evening in as clearly as pulling on a pair of super-comfy pyjama bottoms. And if you're fed up with all the stripes and plaids on offer in the stores, why not whip yourself or your partner up a pair in a fabric that's, um, a little more interesting? We chose an exuberant cowgirl cotton print – but if that sort of thing is beneath your dignity, there are plenty of other options. Just keep away from those boring checks and stripes. Despite the drawstring effect, the trousers are actually elasticated for

Sizing

These bottoms are designed to be a fairly loose fit for a gentleman with an 81–89-cm (32–35-in.) waist. The inside leg measures 81 cm (32 in.), which will be long enough for someone around 1.8 m (6 feet) tall when worn slightly below the natural waistline. You can easily make the bottoms shorter by giving them a bigger hem. You can also make them longer by extending the legs on your template – but remember to allow for extra fabric if you are doing this. You can also use the pattern as a guide for making bottoms in a smaller or larger size, by reducing or expanding the width of the pieces. But there could be a bit of trial and error involved, so make your first pair using some cheap or recycled fabric.

You will need

- ✂ Templates on page 142
- ✂ Tracing paper and paper for templates
- ✂ Pencil
- ✂ 2.5 m (2¾ yd) cotton fabric at least 110 cm (43 in.) wide
- ✂ 1 m (39 in.) red ribbon, 15 mm (⅝ in.) wide
- ✂ 90 cm (1 yd) elastic, 4 cm (1½ in.) wide
- ✂ Thread to match fabric and ribbon
- ✂ Basic sewing kit (see page 4)
- ✂ Large safety pin for threading the elastic

All seam allowances are 1 cm (⅜ in.)

How to make the pyjama bottoms

{1} Prepare your templates following the instructions on page 6 and cut them out.

{2} Cut out two back and two front pieces. Remember to cut one piece of the front and back using your template the right way up and one using your template face down. (If you fold your fabric lengthways before you cut, so that you cut two pieces together, you will automatically cut your pieces correctly.) Cut out two strips to make the waist facing pieces, each measuring 6.5 x 60 cm (2½ x 23½ in.).

{3} Using your sewing machine, zigzag stitch down the sides and crotch curve of all four main pieces.

{4} Pin the two back pieces right sides together and sew the crotch curve. Do the same with the two front pieces. Press all the seams open.

{5} Place one waist facing and the pyjama fronts right sides together, aligning the raw edges at the top. Pin and machine stitch together. Press the seam open. Repeat for the back of the pyjama bottoms, using the second waist facing.

{6} Place the front and back pieces right sides together. Pin down the outside of the legs, matching the seams at the waist facing. Machine stitch together and press the seams open.

{7} Pin down the inside legs, matching the seams at the crotch. Machine stitch together and press the seams open.

{8} Turn under 1 cm (⅜ in.) along the raw edge of the waist facing and press. Turn the facing down and press again. Sew the facing in position as close as possible to the lower folded edge, leaving a 6-cm (2½-in.) gap over one of the side seams for threading the elastic.

{9} Attach the safety pin to one end of the elastic, then thread the elastic through the waistband, taking care that it does not become twisted. Overlap the ends of the elastic and machine or hand stitch them securely together. Close the gap by continuing the line of stitching that holds the waist facing in place.

{10} Turn under 1 cm (⅜ in.) along the raw edge of the legs at the bottom and press. Turn under another 1.5 cm (⅝ in.) and press again. Machine stitch close to the upper folded edge.

{11} Cut the length of red ribbon into two equal pieces. Place the first piece of ribbon on the 'waistband', with one of the raw edges 2.5 cm (1 in.) to the right of the centre and with the main length of the ribbon to the left. Machine stitch close to the raw edge. Flip the ribbon to the right, covering the raw edge, and stitch again, close to the fold, to secure. Sew the other piece of ribbon on the other side. Tie the two lengths of ribbon in a bow.

{2}

{5}

{6}

{8}

{9}

{11}

Templates

Shown at 12.5% – enlarge by 800% for actual size.

Front

Back

114 cm (45 in.)

28 cm (11 in.)

28 cm (11 in.)

Index

A
Advent calendar 76–9
Antarctic play set 55–9
Apple bag 12–16
Apron 100–5

B
baby jacket 128–33
Baby shoes 114–17
backstitch 90
bags 12–16, 110
Bandana bib 85–7
basic sewing kit 4
bias, cutting on 6
bib 85–7
Bird coasters 92–5
boat 50–4
bonding web 5, 6

C
chain stitch 62
Christmas stockings 68–72
clipping corners 7
clipping curves 7
coasters 92–5
cotton fabric 5
cup cosy 88–91

D
Doll-face pillows 38–44
draught buster 80–4

F
Fabric garland 64–7
felt 5
Felt sandals 111–13

F
fibre filling 5
fleece 5, 130
floor cushion 32–8
French knot 58

G
garland 64–7
glue 5

I
iron-on fusible interfacing 5

L
Lavender underwear sachet
 118–21

M
Monster draught buster 80–4

O
oversewing 7

P
Pyjama bottoms 138–42
Phone cosy 29–31
pillows 38–44
pincushion 8–11
play mat 45–9
Pom-pom-trimmed baby jacket
 128–33

R
rabbit 60–3
running stitch 7

S
sandals 111–13
Sarong 106–9
 Travel bag 110
securing stitches 7, 90
Sensory play mat 45–9
Skinny-eared rabbit 60–3
slipstitch 7
Stash box 17–20
Strapped sundress 134–7

T
Table runner 96–9
Tablet case 24–8
tacking 7
tacky glue 5
Take-away cup cosy 88–91
techniques 6–7
templates 6
threads 5
Tomato pincushion 8–11
topstitch 7
tote bag 12–16
Toy boat 50–4
Tree star 73–5

U
underwear sachet 118–21

V
Valentine envelope 21–3

W
wadding 5
Wrap skirt 122–7

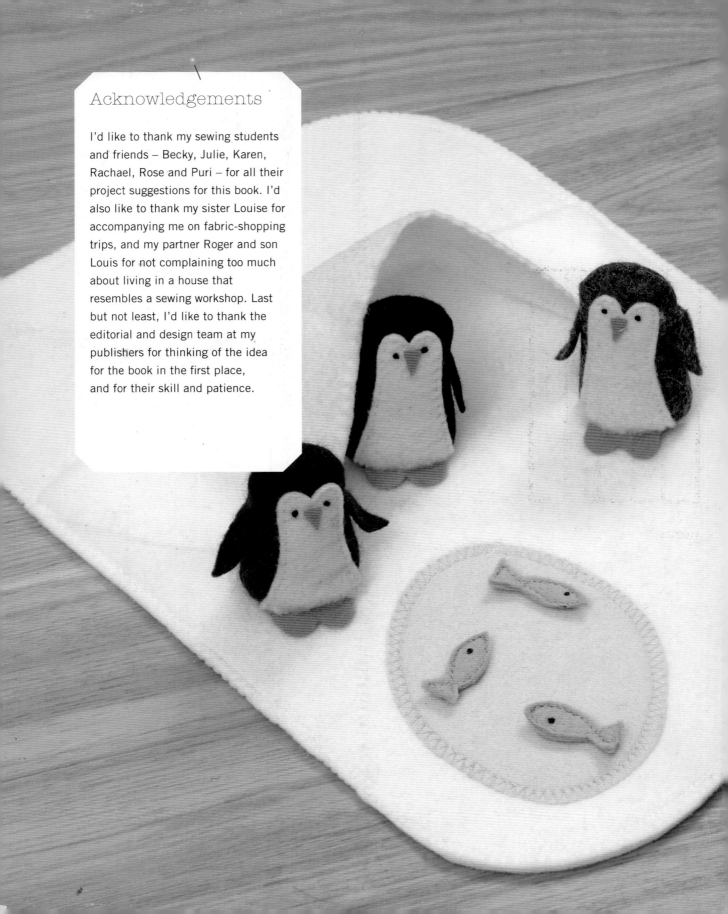

Acknowledgements

I'd like to thank my sewing students and friends – Becky, Julie, Karen, Rachael, Rose and Puri – for all their project suggestions for this book. I'd also like to thank my sister Louise for accompanying me on fabric-shopping trips, and my partner Roger and son Louis for not complaining too much about living in a house that resembles a sewing workshop. Last but not least, I'd like to thank the editorial and design team at my publishers for thinking of the idea for the book in the first place, and for their skill and patience.